The Patterns of Existence

By: Christian Meteor

The Patterns of Existence

ISBN 13: 9781736966303

Copyright © 2021 Christian Meteor

All rights reserved. No part of this book may be reproduced in any form except for the purpose of brief reviews, without written permission of the author.

I give massive gratitude to my love who gave me endless and unconditional support through challenging times. Our story happened in the midst of all of this, and so I promise her that it will be told in the future. I hold great passion for our past in my heart, and so I cannot fully rest until it has been chronicled – for her sake, and mine.

I give love to all of the participants in these stories, no matter which way their paths have gone. The nostalgia of these experiences weighs on me to this day, and so I hope this book can recapture some of those times for both of us.

To my mother who gave me the strength and freedom to live life to the fullest, I am forever grateful. I bring with me unforgettable lessons and abilities that will serve me until the end. I could not have asked for a better mother, nor friend, to understand and guide me through life, to embolden me to live by faith and benevolence.

To Nick for discipline and resolve, who gave me the skills for living my father never could.

All glory to God for the strength he gave me to finish this work, and his divine guidance through difficulty. For his blessings too numerous to count, and unending love.

The Patterns of Existence

Amid a large collection of intensely nostalgic memories, a strong force pushes me to recollect and tell my experiences. Though ideas of modifying these stories to preserve my innocence has proved enticing in the past, I have decided that the truth is entertaining and liberating. I claim what I share is a truthful recollection of the past; however, it is inevitable that my perceptions and biases have been applied to the writing. The perceived meaning and retrospection that I realized from these times is particularly telling. Many of the experiences I had came as a result of me chasing meaning, and so to build a picture and understand the story, this will be a fundamental part.

The true challenge in telling a story is where to begin. The interdependence of events within the chronological universe creates a profound difficulty in providing a thorough understanding of the characters within a story. This is different from a fictitious tale, in which the author can artificially manifest both the beginning and end of a totality. It is the nature of things within our world that inseparable circumstances follow an infinite flow of causality, and as such all details of the cosmos are connected. I would drive myself insane attempting to divulge every aspect of this and its relation to consciousness, and then translate such things into writing. I cannot deny that all details are fundamental because they form the web of matter, but the goal of writing is not to replicate this. Instead, it is to journey to and experience a time frame where a profound set of circumstances is manifested out of the heart of the universe.

On these pages, I have the privilege of walking with you through my past. I am not a guide, rather a fellow voyager, burdened with a heavy curiosity and desire for understanding. Though we do not share the same experiences, we do exist together in a state of perpetual change. As such, our desire to hold onto what has been is mutual, yet there is no way to go back but through an immersive story. These tales are not meant to shock or impress. Instead, I want to experience all of these things with you. I want to feel everything all over again, together.

There is no great reason to tell these stories on a static timeline. Instead, I have pieced together the past based on its perception-altering qualities. In this way, the delayed gratification caused by time can be skipped. The book is then unbound, and evolves not towards a traditional conclusion, but rather as strings to be connected. Therefore, each of these stories comes from different moments in time to not only solve the mystery of nostalgia, but also to clear the fragments of a bleary mirror. As the image reveals itself, the meaning of the refractions will be clarified, but only when the whole picture is unveiled can the delusions be ended and the truth shine through.

Chapter 1

One Day of Senior Year

The February morning was cold and gray outside my urban childhood home, and I was done with my routine, on the way to school. I pushed outside to the driveway with my backpack slung over one shoulder, balancing a mug of hot Earl Grey tea spilling on my hand. It would add to the collection of ceramic cups piling up in my locker, the result of me running late for the past month. Senoritis had come on hard.

Crunchy ice on the driveway battled with the soles of my flat black sneakers as I walked over to my truck. She was shiny red in some spots, and a pale pink in others. Flaking rust plagued her wheel-wells and underbody, and the pungent smell of oil and grime created an aura around her. She had an 8-foot bed with a broken tailgate, and a big Triton V8 motor that ran strong; my first vehicle that I relied on for trips back and forth to school and swim practice during the brutal winter. She even had a little personal touch of a 2-foot scratch and a cracked taillight from the time I had backed into the sycamore on our street.

I nimbly opened the driver side door and lobbed my bag into the passenger seat. The aromas of unburned gasoline and exhaust fumes amplified as I entered the cab, and were trapped as I shut the door. I paused for a moment in the cold silence, letting the reality of the day sink in before bringing the engine to life. She had a moment to warm up while I took sips of the bitter tea that was too hot to guzzle. Then, I revved the motor in park a few times to make a fearsome growl before shifting into drive and coasting off.

    I pushed down the gas pedal, soaring to the end of the icy street to pick up my friend. I slowed down a few houses from his, and noticed some familiar details along the road. The first to catch my eye was a divet in the snow down to the asphalt. This bore the shape of an upright wheel, and pointed towards tire tracks and the indent of the front end of a car on the snowy curb. Bits of plastic and frozen clumps of sand dotted the road and I could not help but giggle at my memory of the previous night.

    I parked outside Slater's house and tapped my horn a few times. A couple minutes of impatient waiting later, I watched him laze out of the snow-covered house and lock the door. He had a sleek form and squinty pale blue eyes that were glazed over from his ritualistic morning bake session. His pasty-white skin almost blended with curly blonde hair, and a familiar sly grin grew as he got closer to the truck. He opened the passenger door, and I met him with a "Yo."

    "Hey, fucker, you made my dad real suspicious last night" he said.

    "If you hadn't made me drive you home after dabbing and had just walked your lazy ass two blocks, that wouldn't have happened." I retorted.

"What the hell did you even do last night?" he asked, shutting the door.

"After I dropped you off, I tried to clear the curb with my truck instead of multi pointing the backup," I started until breaking with laughter at my own actions.

"Well, that was a great idea!" he yelled.

"I've done it before but never on dabs. Or in the winter. It wasn't the best choice." I could not help but to continue laughing at the mess I'd created. Evidence of high shenanigans littered Slater's road, and I eased off slowly to take it all in.

"Anyway, when I realized I couldn't make it over the curb, I put my truck in reverse and punched the gas pedal which made a rut in the snow on the road. The truck wouldn't move, as each time I put it into drive, it just ended up further in the snowbank. I tried putting it into reverse, but that just made the rut bigger."

We started out onto the main road, passing the local liquor store decorated with a big barrel banner. This was right across the street from the grocery store where Slater worked.

"So, I figured I'd go ahead and use some of the play sand I keep in the bed on the wheels to try to get some traction."

"Yeah, that's what I would have done."

"Well, little did I know that sand just turns into a

block under twenty degrees. I first tried using my ice scraper to cut open the bag which just broke the cheap plastic. Then, I figured I'd bust the bag open, so I stood in the truck bed and chucked the block down onto the concrete."

"I can see your ass out there in the middle of the night, high as fuck, just smashing a bag of sand against the road."

"I figured it was the best choice at that point."

We turned at the familiar intersection marked by the indoor smoking quickstop, a fish chicken place that went out of business every other year, the public library, and an ice cream store that had changed ownership a dozen times.

"So I helplessly tried using the sandbag which did absolutely nothing." I told him. I remembered kicking a block of sand out of sheer anger and numbing my toe, but figured I would spare him that detail. "That's when I came and knocked on your window and told you that I was stuck."

"I went and got my dad and then some shovels. When you were gone he must have thought I was tripping," Slater replied.

"Man, all I could think about was how I was going to have to leave my truck there overnight and walk home. Not to mention how clear it was that I had tried to drive over the curb like an idiot. I figured you were my last hope."

Continuing down the straight road to school, we passed familiar houses and a park that I'd walked hundreds of times.

"Well, I managed to get out when I made a big indent in the road by going forwards and backwards. Eventually, the snowbank was compressed enough that I could get the speed to get out. I felt such a wave of relief when I was finally driving down your road towards home." I concluded.

"That's crazy, man. You just left all that stuff on the road too, huh?" he asked. I could not help but laugh more.

"Yup, I just wanted to get home."

Our morning commute came to a close as we arrived at school, and though more would come, this one was done. Now was time to begin the day and work our way through the final semester of high school classwork. I paid no special attention to this particular day; it is merely a humorous story that Slater and I had shared. To me, it was a reason to never dab and drive, though I broke that rule many more times: To Slater, perhaps it was just another day of tomfoolery with his high school friend.

Regardless of what either of us felt after that day, I never could have guessed how much a simple and seemingly trivial event would weigh upon me. Perhaps that sentiment is not experience exclusive, rather a nostalgia for **all** that was happening in that time. Slater was my best friend, and we shared countless meaningful times together in this era. Without him, senior year would have been far less unique-he brought out in me a blissful apathy. He taught me to not take things too seriously, to be easy on myself, and to embrace the path of revelry-for better and for worse.

Chapter 2

Sugar, Oil, and Fire

The summer night air poured in through the windows of Heub's black Jeep. He drove while Bo sat passenger side and I got to control the mp3 station from the back. We were bored and desperate, looking for fun despite sobriety and teenage malaise. Our standard was high; we had been pranking together for years. Ding-dong-ditching, tp-ing, and laser pointers in neighbors windows brought us great joy at the expense of others. The closer we got to graduating high school, the more intense our pranks got, as did the threshold for a fun night. That was all behind us now, though. Graduation was months in the past, yet here we were, driving around aimlessly, trying to hatch up a plan for the evening.

The three of us were pretty similar; 160-pound, lean framed 17 year olds with impetuous dispositions. Heubert had ginger brown, crew cut hair with a rounded nose, pasty white complexion, freckles, and guilty eyes. Rarely could you catch him frowning. Bo had a tan complexion with long lashes above blue eyes. His hair was moppy and dirty blonde atop a narrow face, and he usually wore a subtly wistful expression except when in the midst of hooliganism or novelty. Then there was me with platinum blonde, split ended, and lengthy hair, bleached by the chlorine of a pool. Dark blue eyes, a freckle just above my lip, and my dad's heroic jawline.

We cruised by high school, former classmates' houses, and ever so familiar points in space. There was no reminiscence on this night. No talk of our times shared in highschool or the incredible series of events that had led us up to this particular point. The only focus was on having fun. Senior summer was here, and though none of us knew exactly when or how we would go our separate ways, we understood it was inevitable, even in our naive youth. Now was the time to make memories, lest the night go unfilled, and be lost to the many others we had shared.

The moon rose high into the dark sky as we carelessly emitted and devised plans for a thrill. Nothing in the realm of hooliganism was off the table. Tp-ing and doughnutting were our most utilized methods of bringing strife into the lives of those with whom we had a score to settle. The rush of trespassing in the dark of night was unparalleled, as was the joy of leaving debris on the lawns and houses of kids we knew. Our primary reference was the old school phonebook, where we had access to all the addresses of our classmates. Our secondary source was word of mouth: where we had friends on our sports teams or extracurricular activities who had the desired information.

We cackled at the thought of our schoolmates waking up to a house blanketed in bleached white strands of single-ply. The cheapest toilet paper was the best choice not only because we were poor highschoolers, but also because of its unique property of disintegrating into unretrievable pieces. Even then, enough paper to cover a house was still expensive, and a more economic option was to raid the local doughnut chain dumpster. Once again, we jovially toyed with thoughts of claiming the cars and yards of students by gifting them soggy dough rings saturated with fry oil and sugar that had been melted by the summer heat.

The memories of these times were, unfortunately, better than any plans for future ones, and an unmistakable sadness existed within all of us that would not allow itself to be revealed. The fact of the matter was, high school was over. The satisfaction that lay in hearing rumours around school of someone who got tped would never come. Our class had moved on and would never go back, but here we were, clinging to the past. Whether we held onto our fading delinquent ideologies in an attempt to relive all of our glorious weekends together, or to simply get a thrill, there was no question that we fought hard against the looming change.

As the green digital clock on the dashboard got closer to midnight, our urgency grew. The night would come to a close within the next three hours, and if we did not do something soon, it would be wasted. We made a unanimous decision to pay a visit to the local doughnut chains dumpster and scope out a nice big bag. We did not exactly have a plan for what to do with it, but having been through this ritual a dozen times before, we had no doubt it would be given some purpose. The doughnut shop was located on the corner of two busy streets with a large shopping center behind it. At first glance, this would seem to be a terrible location to attempt a dumpster dive, but this fact worked in our favour. We blended in with traffic, and there were multiple escape routes to main roads from the store.

Heub was always cautious when approaching situations such as these, much the opposite of Bo. Heub was often the voice of reason, presenting worst case scenarios, and offering discouragement when the situation was not ideal. Bo, on the other hand, was reckless. He had little to no concern with being caught and focused primarily on the fun of the adventure. There was no room for worry with him, merely a straight path to completing the prank. I assumed the role of mediary between the differing approaches. With the three of us, there was no room for ties. I am convinced that had it only been Heub and I, no pranks would have been completed; and had it been only Bo and I, we most certainly would have been caught red handed.

As we approached the doughnut shop, the heart pounding thrill of what we were about to do was ever so weaker than it had been before. Heub pulled the car up a few paces away from the dumpster and parked close for a quick plunder and getaway. Tonight was Bo's turn to get the doughnuts; he and I would alternate the role of watcher and carrier for this stunt while Heub was always the driver. The two of us gingerly got out of the car and walked as casually as we could to a dumpster filled with doughnuts at midnight. The gate was unlocked, and I stood watch while ushering Bo into the brick cube surrounding the disturbingly large green cans. I kept my eyes peeled on the back door of the shop where employees periodically brought out trash, and within seconds, Bo was hissing "go, go, go!"

I quickly sprinted away from the trash can, feeling an immense sense of vulnerability and a burning down my spine. I turned around once I was a short distance from the car and saw Bo hauling a 60-pound bag of greasy doughnuts. As long as no one saw us in this short window of time, we would be in the clear. Once Bo was just over halfway to the car, the plastic bottom of the bag began to sag like a full diaper and eventually ripped. His expression changed from urgency to disregard as he dropped the bag in the middle of the lot and ran over to the car. We both jumped in and Heub immediately asked, "Did you get them?"

"No, the bag tore and I didn't want it to get all over your car," Bo immediately responded.

" What are we going to do now? Just leave it?" I asked as we began heading towards the main street. "We could try to get another one."

"That was the only one in there, dude," Bo said.

In that moment, a small tube caught my eye on the floor of the car, and a brilliant idea came to mind.

"What if we lit this artillery shell in it?" I asked excitedly.

There was silence for a moment, followed by a curt statement from Bo. "Okay, but you do it."

Before Heub or reason could weigh in, I grabbed

the firework and ran out of the car towards the pathetic bag of fat and sugar. I quickly stuffed the shell a few inches into the doughnuts, and held a red lighter flame to the fuse. That particular moment felt like eternity, until the fuse flared to life, and set in place a countdown until a colorfully criminal explosion. Within seconds I was slamming the door to the back seat, watching out the rear windshield as Heub sped away from the scene. An eruption of purple sparks and doughnut chunks filled the sky for a brief, legendary second, followed by a steady fire that enveloped the bag.

We howled in laughter as Heub gunned it out of the parking lot onto the main road.

"That thing was still on fire!" Bo announced.

"I can't believe you just did that," Heub said.

"We gotta see if it keeps burning!" Bo insisted. "Turn up here into this gas station."

Making a completely inconspicuous turn, we pulled into a spot and collected ourselves for a brief moment. The infiltration, the doughnuts and the explosion-it all happened so fast. We could not reveal even a sliver of suspicion though; we had to be just three guys grabbing some soda.

"Do you guys want anything?" Heub asked.

"I'm good for now," I answered while Bo was already getting out of the car to head in. I watched the two of them select sugary beverages and sheepishly pay the attendant. I looked directly at Heub as he walked out of the store with a guilty smirk on his face and a green Monster in hand. Bo followed soon after, guzzling a Mountain Dew Black Label as he pushed open the door.

A brief silence after the two of them entered the car was broken by Heub cracking his beverage and asking: "You guys want to go see if it's still burning?"

Bo and I jinxed each other with a definitive yes, and soon we were pulling back out onto the main road. We took our time getting up to speed until the smoldering bag was in clear view.

"It's still going!" Bo exclaimed as Heub increased speed, leading us away from the grease fire.

I watched from the back seat as the fire drew further from view before scanning for any witnesses. We seemed to be in the clear, so I lazed into the seat with a big smile and slight feeling of guilt and responsibility. I mean, no one was dumb enough to drive their car over a fire in the street, right? I just hoped the security cameras didn't catch us. Perhaps the most vile part was the pollution; what a terrible thing to spew into the environment. Still, that was awesome.

Before I knew it, we were pulling up outside the large sycamore near my house. Both of my friends' beverages were gone, and it was time to go in for the night. We quietly entered the house and whispered about how long the bag would burn before ruling the night a success. I prepared sleeping arrangements which consisted of a mattress pulled out from underneath my bed and a big leather couch in the living room. I gathered some extra pillows and blankets for my friends, and then the three of us were off asleep for the night.

Little did I know, not only would this be the last time we would steal doughnuts together, but it also would be one of the last times I rode around aimlessly at night with them, searching for fun. If someone had told me that it would be the last time, I would not have believed them. I never thought much about the future, only the times we had together. So much had changed since our first nights of foolish adventure together, and what seemed like trivial times that would be shared indefinitely, soon were left to the past.

The profound difference I find from being in the midst of those times, and reflecting upon them, is the great sentiment I have attached to their simplicity. What once was just another night with my friends is now a potent memory of experiences I can never go back to, but in thought.

Chapter 3

Wilx Park

While biking home from school on a mild spring afternoon, the damp air saturated my lungs and glazed my skin. I had plans with two of my sophomore friends, Slater and Max. They were going to pick me up at home and then head to a park near Max's house on the other side of town. These guys had been my buddies for over five years, and so it seemed like a fun way to spend a Friday night. Once I made it home from school, I told my mom that I was going to the park to play frisbee and then video games after with friends. She gave me the usual motherly monologue to be careful, but had no reason to be suspicious.

That feeling of coming home from school on a Friday was a fine blend of relief and excitement. Not only would I have some freedom from the repetitive grind, but also time for video games and debaucherous activity with friends. Spring made it all that much sweeter, as I was finished with four months of swimming six days a week, and would not have to wake up early tomorrow and jump into a cold pool for three hours. Winter was gone, and glorious spring weather was here, ripe for adventure and longboarding.

I was a bit nervous though. Slater would be driving and almost all of my time in a car had been spent with my mom and grandma. I did have a learners permit that gave me an awareness of what was happening on the road, but ultimately my life would be in the hands of my friend. He gave me no reason to distrust him and had demonstrated proficiency in the past, but I figured it only natural to have an underlying sense of caution.

    I impatiently waited at the window until I saw my friends roll up across the street in a white 2001 Honda Civic. I jumped out onto the porch of my snug home and made my way over to the car. Opening the door, I noted how thin the metal was, and the small back seat. A crash in this vehicle meant certain demise for all of us, and a looming thought of being trapped invaded my mind. I tried to ignore it, and soon the three of us were heading down my street, tunneled by the lime green canopy of thick trees.

    Slater sat in the driver's seat wearing a white athletic quarter zip and black sport shades. Above them, short blonde hair fell into small curls, and his cheeks were rosy red against skin bleached white from the winter months. Max sat passenger side with a similar rosy cheeked appearance and sleek brown hair that reached forward to the top of his cheekbones. We all had slender statures and attitudes of indolence, perfectly aligning with the stigma of rebellious teenage boys.

    The only thing I had brought was a frisbee, no wallet, pocketknife, water bottle, phone, or key. I had no worries of having money to buy food, or a method to call home if something went wrong. I was just focused on the moment, entirely unaware of the potential dangers that could sprout from the world. I had next to no forethought or planning for the evening, just common sense in terms of danger; vulnerable to far more than I knew.

    Slater navigated afterschool traffic as we made our way down the straight road to the east side of town. I did not have a great sense of direction, but eventually we came upon a familiar area that brought up memories of time spent with my god brother. I could not see exactly where we were, but the roads were recognizable and brought warm memories of climbing fences and trees with him. This warm feeling was soon met with an unsettling recollection of the two of us rolling chestnuts out into the road and watching them be crushed by cars, followed by an angry man storming out of his vehicle after us.

    The nostalgia was absent from these memories, replaced by a simple feeling of fondness. I had built my understanding of where I was upon them, and though I did not know how I had gotten here, I knew I had been here before. I also knew that the road would soon come to a hill that led down to a pretentious part of town, and that my dad's house was just at the top of that hill. I left that thought, and chose to tune into the discussion between Slater and Max about our plans for the evening.

    "So we're just going to meet him there, then?" Slater asked.

    "Yeah, he lives right by the park. He's just going to walk over," Max replied.

"Isn't that kind of sketch?" Slater asked.

"No man, It'll be fine." Max answered.

"Who are we meeting?" I asked.

"Oh, no one; Max is just going to meet him," Slater quickly replied, "It's his neighbor." I did not know what kinds of friends Max had around home, or the people he knew at this park, so I paid little mind to it. I still wondered why it was just Max meeting him though, and how Slater knew him.

Cruising down the straight stretch of road through the bougie part of town, Slater carefully monitored his speed and made sure to completely stop at each sign. He was as well aware as I that the police around here did not take kindly to unfamiliar faces. The houses here were huge with yards three times as big, manicured to a tee. I recalled driving down these streets on Christmas Eve, when the snowy roads were artfully lined with bags of candles; something I had only seen on this part of town.

Max began giving directions as the road became unfamiliar, and soon, we reached the edge of the pompous municipality. The change in scenery was rather drastic. The houses were hundreds of years older and colored with vibrant pastels and unique architecture. The lawns were no longer flat and freshly mowed; instead, they were filled with blooming spring bushes and climbing over pergolas and up lattices. The vibe was informal and a bit novel; this place felt like it had more magic and alternative behavior than where I came from.

    Shortly after entering the new part of town, we were turning down a side street littered with potholes to Wilx park. Young people dressed in bohemian apparel drifted carelessly around the green space, stringing up hammocks and forming sitting circles atop falsa blankets. A forested area lined the back of a green valley with occasional trails leading down into concealed areas. This part was separated from a two acre field by two large tennis courts and weathered picnic tables. At the other end of the field, a small playground sat a short ways from a dilapidated bathroom, propped up against more brush. The entire park seemed narrow against the sidewalk, but I wondered how deep the forest went.

    Slater parked the car near the tennis courts where the road curved, and the three of us headed out into the field. Once we had formed a triangle, we passed the frisbee around trying nontraditional catches and throws. There was something very satisfying about watching the disc glide effortlessly through the air into the hands of my friends. With every successful catch, we would attempt a more difficult one. Long distance hucks, running predictions, and forehands were the most fun and the most failed. Smiles and shouts dominated the activity paired with light hearted harassment and an overall casual vibe.

    I had been trading throws with Slater when I

noticed Max split off from the triangle and head toward the playground. I caught one more and closed the gap with Slater before asking "Where's he going?"

"He's going to meet his buddy. He'll be back in a minute," Slater replied earnestly.

"What's he doing?" I asked.

"Buyin' some weed," Slater answered.

I stared at him for a second and then turned to see Max headed towards a black sedan that had just parked on the edge of the street. He looked around casually and then slinked into the front seat, shutting the door.

"Let's go wait for him." Slater said, heading towards the playground set back from the road.

Once we had crossed the field, I went to hang from the monkey bars and watch the car. With no drug dealer experience, I wondered if this was going to be the last time I would ever see my friend. The only thing I knew about them was the cultural stigmatization that they were low life villains who would pull a gun out and rob you, or worse.

"How much is he getting?" I asked Slater.

"Just a couple grams." he said as Max exited the vehicle and began heading our way. It was at this moment that I saw him differently. Who had once been my innocent childhood friend was now exiting a drug deal, walking straight towards me. I felt a certain degree of liability and involvement too, even though I had no intention of smoking. Not only was the guy fresh off a drug deal clearly my associate, but his house was the only safe place on this side of town. I began to doubt the evening I had planned, and with Slater as my only way home, I felt stuck and burdened with whatever my friends were doing.

"You got it?" Slater asked.

"Yeah, let's go to the void. I'll show you," Max said as he walked past us, heading back towards the tennis courts. Slater followed while I lagged back a bit, cautious about what was happening. I knew they were going to smoke and I was not interested in getting busted, but remained curious about how they were going to do it. My only prior experience with weed was the first time I had ever seen it; that was here in Wilx park a few months ago. An honest longboard trip with my middle school friend Kode and a few classmates had turned into a northern lights blunt burning session. I made sure to stay a safe distance away from the incredibly immoral act, and then assumed the role of mother hen for my intoxicated classmates as they raced down asphalt.

Behind the tennis courts was a dirt path that led down a hill through underbrush. The two of them ducked in, and I followed, wondering how a place could live up to the name of "void." After a short walk along a rooty path, the brush opened into a clearing with a large dead tree covered with different colors of graffiti. The trunk stretched three feet wide with holes bored into old branch nodes that were speckled with cigarette butts and cigar wrappers. A few empty beer cans were stuck in the mud surrounding dry ground, and a boggy thicket expanded out behind the tree. We were concealed in all directions, and I then understood why this was the preferred spot.

    Slater and Max both knew that I had no interest in smoking, and when they began preparing, I took a few steps away. I saw a tiny plastic bag with small green clumps wadded up in it, and a little piece of blue and white glass. I tried to make it appear as if I was uninvolved in what they were doing, but craned my neck in an attempt to see. Soon, a sour odor tickled my nose and I instantly noted the unique aroma. I had never smelled fresh weed before and it smelled felonious but magical, like a mix of foreign land and organic gasoline.

    Max wasted no time and brought the glass to his mouth, torching the bowl. He took one big inhale and held it for a few seconds before blowing out a wispy trail. Coughing and smiling, he passed the piece to Slater while I kept my distance, dodging the fumes. This evening had already become more precarious than I was comfortable with and I even began to feel a tightness in my chest and a subtle burning in my stomach.

    Slater then took a puff off of the glass, blowing out the smoke a few seconds later. He began to cough weakly and closed his eyes while Max cackled and wheezed. Then I watched Slater bend over with his hands and his knees and spit towards the ground, remarking that this was only his third time smoking. Seconds after, he was forced to regain his composure as his phone rang and it was his mother. I could not believe the incredibly unfortunate timing of this call, and I watched helplessly as he attempted to act calm and not give away his actions immediately preceding this call.

The call lasted a few painful minutes while Max and I kept silent before Slater tucked his phone into his back pocket and stated, "That was messed up." I sympathized with him while Max laughed and bounced around until all of our attention was taken to a rustling in the bushes up the hill. I could have sworn in that exact moment that federal agents in black suits were going to come busting out, taking all of us into custody.

Frozen in place, I watched as three large people emerged from the thick bushes, and I soon recognized who it was: Kode and crew.

Kode was a heavy set boy with dark umber skin and a head full of tightly wound, pencil-size dreadlocks going every direction. He and two of his friends I did not recognize came lumbering down the hill towards us, carrying backpacks and a suspicious aura. I was by no means settled, but temporarily relieved from the fear of police.

"Hey, what are you guys doing?" Kode asked as the three of them made it to the bottom of the hill into the void.

"We just smoked," Max answered while walking over and performing a special handshake with each of the new arrivals. It became apparent at this point that this was not happenstance; these people had been told about where we would be. I was not made aware of this, and I did not think Slater was either.

"Y'all got a whip?" Kode asked, to which Slater answered with a nod. A car was a great asset at this age and allowed for an immense amount of freedom for both you and friends.

"Can you give us a ride to Wing Road?" Kode asked. Slater paused for a moment; before answering, he was interrupted by Max.

"It's just a couple blocks down."

I sympathized with the pressure on Slater and with four against one, he said yes. Even though this was most certainly not the plan for the evening, saying no would have brought pushback and disappointment. I did not think Slater was capable of saying no in his intoxicated state, and so we all began heading up the bumpy root path.

At this time, the reality of what was happening began to sink in for me. My friend was on drugs and was about to drive a bunch of people in a small sedan. This was everything I was told not to do in drivers training and horror stories permeated my mind. Dead kids who drove under the influence-that was the impending doom that awaited all of us. The less obvious and smart solution was to make these guys walk to where they needed to go. Then Slater could come down to take me home, where I dearly desired to be. Peer pressure, however, demanded that we all get in the car and get to the destination.

    I decided that the next best option was for me to drive. This was entirely illegal on a learner's permit without an adult, not to mention I did not have it with me. There were also restrictions on the number of people you could have in the car, and I knew for a fact that six was too many. I did not want to do it, but I knew it was the right choice. I had no clue where Wing Road was, but as long as it was close, I figured I could make it a few blocks to drop these guys off. Then all I would have to do is drive the short distance to Max's house and either spend the night or at least let Slater sober up.

    I hopped in the driver's seat and Slater got into the passenger seat. Then, I felt the car sink as the four guys piled into the back, squished together in one big dog pile.

    "Ready to go?" Slater asked, looking carefully at me. I answered by turning the keys in the ignition and accepting the great risk. I deemed it safer than letting my friend drive under the influence and getting into an accident, so after staring at the shifter for a moment, I put it in drive. I slowly let my foot off the brake, and to my great surprise, the car began to move. I took it slowly out of the parking spot and then Max began hollering directions from the back as I neared the end of the street.

The four of them were squirming around a lot, and I figured it was quite uncomfortable dealing with everybody butting shoulders. I brought the car to a halt at the first stop sign and looked into the rear view mirror, checking to see if there were any cops or people that would identify the delinquents in this car. No police; instead, what I saw was Kode sitting in the middle seat holding a backpack in front of him with a fifth of vodka poking out of the top. I noticed a quarter of it was gone as he pulled it out and was passing it between his friends. I could not believe the insane amount of a liability; not only was I driving illegally, but now there was an open container in the car.

I was furious at Kode for his reckless action and disregard, but figured I would be rid of him and his thug friends soon. I only had to suffer a few streets of paranoid driving before pulling into the pizza place when they wanted to be let out. All four of them filed out of the back of the car; their strut was dull and eyes half open. Max went along with them and made it clear that he was done hanging out with us today. I was disappointed and unhappy with my friend; Slater and I had been ditched and now had to find our way back across town to get home.

I had no idea where I was going but did not trust Slater to navigate high, so I just used my best judgment to find the way back. I pulled out of the parking lot onto the bumpy side roads, remaining anxious and fearful of being caught by the police. I had only gone a short ways before peering into the side view-mirror and seeing a black SUV pull out of a driveway. A sick feeling that someone was watching us infiltrated my mind and quickly I began heading in the direction I thought was home. Less than a minute had passed before I saw the same black SUV pull out of a hidden side street, causing my heart to drop. I quickly took a left at the next available street and was focusing intently on the road until Slater casually stated, "Hey, buddy, you're going down a one way." I was shocked at this fact that was confirmed by every single car facing the other way. Things today just kept going bad and I gave great thanks that no police had seen us, and that no other cars had been traveling down the road at this moment. I turned off at the next available street and parked on the side of the road.

"Can you drive, Slater?" I asked sincerely.

"Yeah, man, I'm good now."

A wave of relief filled with shards of doubt washed over me as we hopped out of the car and switched places. The evening was not over: I still had to place my trust in Slater's intoxicated driving skills. It was just slow streets to take home and Slater knew his way back, so I figured we had a good shot, but death still loomed.

I spotted the street sign and I could not believe my eyes: Benos Street.

"We are on BENOS STREET man!" I shouted at Slater.

"Well, that's fucking great!" he said, matching my tone as we turned off of the dangerous road.

"We're lucky we didn't get shot!" Slater offered half jokingly. I remained in disbelief of the place I had decided to get out of the car. This street was notorious for gang activity and shootings, and we two private Christian school boys were dancing around our car on it.

I once again gave thanks for my safety, and watched Slater and the road closely as he cautiously cruised through the neighborhood. His driving was much better than expected, but I would check in every couple minutes in case I needed to take over.

Once we were less than ten minutes from home, I was watching the light on the horizon when Slater had the audacity to offer to drive us to the grocery store for spicy corn tortilla snacks. I shook my head in disbelief. I had absolutely no interest in remaining in the car with a drugged driver longer than I had to. I just wanted to get home safely and tell my mom about everything that happened. Between the waves of emotions, levels of liability, and my perception of Kode and Max being forever changed, I had a story to tell. School brought me together with these guys, but I was now made well aware of their risky behavior and the degree of danger I faced when tagging along with them.

Dusk had just begun to set in as Slater pulled up outside of my house. I leaned back into the seat with a heavy sigh before opening the door and giving Slater one last look.

"Thanks for getting me home safe. You should head back now too."

"Of course; I'm good, man. I'm going to hit up the store for some munchies before though."

"You should go home, dude. It's not safe to drive high, especially without someone watching." I insisted. He nodded at me but I knew his plan for the evening still included a trip to the grocery store and I wondered if it was going to be the last time I would ever see him. I said farewell and gave his fate to the creator before stepping out onto the grass and watching him drive off. I was so thankful to be home safely, and as I walked up to my front porch, my mom opened the door and invited me in. I hugged her tight and felt safe; I knew I could go into detail about what had happened that evening without fear of any punishment. I was so happy to have her to share with and come home to. My evening had been terrifying, and now I was safely home, ready to savor peace and stability.

Chapter 4

Interior Vapor

The night began with Bo and me in the back seat of Heub's black Jeep, celebrating with Slater for his 18th birthday. I knew that tagging along with these fellows would bring some sort of delinquent activity, be it drug consumption or disregard for the law. I had direct exposure to Slater and Bo's transition into the realm of drugs over the past two years, as they were two of my closest friends. I chose not to partake in their use of weed and other forms of dope, but that did not get in the way of our friendship. They understood that I would not tolerate peer pressure, but that I was happy to tag along, even if it meant I did not join them for recreational use.

My friends had been discussing how they had gone about acquiring weed this evening, and their success. I knew by the aroma coming off of Slater that they were not joking, and I soon had my curiosity piqued as he pulled out a large mason jar filled with mysterious gold and green nuggets. I figured I would have a close look at something novel tonight, but no forethought could have prepared me for the outlandish feelings connected to this setting. I was just outside the door to an entirely new world of people and motives. Secretive deals and dark night car rides burned feelings of depravity and sheer wonder in me at the immense amount of hype built around marijuana. So, too, did past exposure to the media heighten my curiosity as saturated colors, descriptions of strange headspaces, and overexaggerated visual effects all tempted me closer to some kind of mystical weed experience.

My mind played games as Slater began loading up a glass tube. He turned around towards me from the passenger seat, and brashly stated: "Alright man, it's my 18th birthday. I'm not going to pressure you into it. I'm not going to make you do it, but we're going to hotbox a little bit."

I nodded as excitement began to grow in me. Even though in this specific moment I had not decided if I was going to break my years of abstinence, I still had a great curiosity in me. I longed to smell it and I wanted to see it. I wanted to see my friends do it, and I wanted to be a part of it. The idea of trying it became more and more real by the second, and soon the vaporizer had been passed to Bo right next to me. Sweet pungent aroma aroused my nostrils as the car filled with a scent of caramelized trichomes, and soon the desire to taste what my friends were tasting became insatiable. The atmosphere was especially unique. The enveloping dark cabin, the orange lights of the dashboard, four friends, and a day that would only happen once.

Bo looked at me holding out the vaporizer and said "Do you want to try it?"

By this point, I had made the decision, and so I uttered a "yes." A brief moment of comfortably hidden surprise surged through my friends as they spared me heckling and dissuasion attempts. A silent few seconds passed while I took a long inhale out of the tube and then lazed back into my seat as I exhaled. My mind began adding it up, and I soon realized that I had done it. I had just consumed marijuana for the first time, and could never go back to where I had been.

Eager to see what effects would come, I tried to focus on what I was feeling and see if I could identify any discernible differences. I knew it would take some time before I could feel the effects, yet I was still reveling in the fact that I had just used weed for the first time. Caught up in my thoughts, I soon heard the silence of the car break with the ignition of the engine. I did not know where we were going, and I was not feeling anything yet, but the pure facts of the night elevated my mood. I was truly in the moment with my friends.

Our first destination was a CVS pharmacy just down the road from my house to get some snacks. As the four of us entered the store, I had no worries of being identified as a cannabis user, or appearing high. I simply walked with my friends to the back of the store and stared at the huge variety of colors in the chip aisle. In these moments, I did not feel high. The only noticeable effect was my inability to remove a smile from my face for the entirety of my time in the store.

A subtle haze seemed to float in the atmosphere of that store, as specific details were not apparent, and my focus was on the effects of marijuana on my consciousness.

The unique aspect of this time was the stark duality of familiarity. I had been in this location so many times in the past, yet in this moment it felt strange. The ceiling seemed oddly high and I noticed parts of the store I had never looked closely at. Little did I know that my perception of the entire external world could be radically changed by small shifts in my mind.

Our short but peculiar time in CVS came and went as my friends acquired beverages and snacks. We returned to the car and then headed to a gas station that was well known for its glass and low prices. Seeing as Slater had just turned 18, he planned to buy his first bubbler to amp up consumption for the evening. The amount of alcohol, tobacco, and prescription drugs he had consumed before becoming an "adult" made today oddly more special than if he had never done anything. He had already been an addict for over a year; what in the hell would being *legally* allowed to purchase nicotine bring?

Though we all had school tomorrow, the night was young, and the intent was to celebrate Slater's birthday. The unchanging fact that these moments were exclusive to this specific time was not consciously apparent, but I still knew that these minutes were precious. I did not have an understanding of the fleeting nature of reality then, and as such my mind was ruffled by the vagaries of things that were not happening in that moment. It was as if my material presence with my friends was competing against a growing seed of preoccupation in my mind. Time would show that this was merely a battle in the war of my thoughts and assumptions that were to come. If I had been made aware of the degree of intensity my future experiences would hold, I would have savored these moments, and found humor in the comparatively easy challenges I faced then.

    I stared out the window as dim yellow street lights passed by creating spheres of amber glow on the pavement. Overhearing Slater give Heub directions to our destination, I struggled to gain a sense of where I was. An underlying feeling of change stirred about in my mind as I thought about all of the times I had been offered weed in the past. I felt proud of my firm resilience to it, but wondered if any of it meant anything now that I had consumed. I did not know what my ego was at this time, but I knew that I had lost a bragging right and differentiating factor from me and my friends. My false sense of superiority over people who used was gone, and I now was what I had judged in the past. Instead of feeling like I was isolated and different from people who smoked weed, I felt I was one of them.

    Time had flown by when I noticed that we were pulling underneath a tall gas station shelter, lit up by fluorescent white lights and bright red paint. As Heub brought the car to a park and silenced the engine, the four of us sat briefly for a moment. I gazed into the gas station and identified a large rectangular glass case in front of a cash register, set a short ways away from a tall wall filled with colorful tobacco brands. A slender Indian man in his 20s with striking hair was behind the register, looking longfully out into the night. I wondered how this guy would receive four teenage boys coming into his store, and then noticed all of my friends were getting out of the car. I thought about staying to avoid a potentially uncomfortable experience, but curiosity about the glass bongs got the best of me, so I hopped out, and followed them in.

    Slater immediately walked up to the glass case while Bo, Heub, and I hung back, poking around the store. Neither Bo nor I were 18 yet, and so we did not want to appear as if we were going to be partaking in the activities of our friends who were a couple months older. I was looking at some sugary treats, reminiscing about how our high school used to sell them, when I noticed Slater inspecting a little glass bubbler held by the clerk. This was perhaps the first time I had felt weed paranoia, as it seemed very evident to me that the clerk knew that the purpose of this purchase was to get these four high school boys high.

    After a few uncomfortable minutes, Slater pulled out his wallet and showed his ID. The clerk looked at it and then handed it back, informing him that he could not purchase this item until the day following his birthday. Slater then coaxed Heub over to buy the bubbler for him, and in this particular moment, the success of our journey depended on Heub. Following the transaction that most definitely had a suspicious feeling, the four of us quickly left the store and piled back into the car.

    "Where to now?" Heub asked.

"We could go smoke in a park," Bo answered.

"No, that's way too sketchy. Let's go to someone's place," Slater said.

"Not my house," Heub replied. "My parents would be very sus."

"Not my house either," Bo stated.

"We never go to your house," Slater contended.

"That's because of my parents," Bo retorted.

"Everyone has parents, Bo." Heub pressured him.

A short silence followed, broken by Slater asking, "What about your house, Christian?"

I thought for a moment, and figured it was late enough that my mom had gone to sleep. My garage was private with some seats and a stereo, and it seemed like an ideal location to get high with my friends. This was also a great birthday present for Slater: a smoke spot.

I answered, "Sure," causing the mood of the entire car to brighten. The idea of a classic affair in a garage brought teenage delight and excitement, and soon, we were all heading off to my house. I was quite eager to experience a true first smoke session, and I believe that my friends wanted to give me a superb first experience with weed that would never be forgotten.

Heub parked in front of my house on this dark night,

and then the four of us hopped out of the car. I led the crew up my cobble driveway towards the garage, followed by Slater with a black backpack slung over his shoulder. Heub and Bo followed close behind, speaking softly about the activities that were to come. With my friends gathered around me, I flipped a switch on the front of the garage and then slipped my fingers under the rubber bottom of the door, attempting to pull it up with as little sound as possible.

The clamorous metal bearings broke the silence of the night while light from the garage shone out into the driveway, revealing four scrawny teenage boys. There we were, looking into the perfect place to smoke. Bundles of tools littered the wall and dumbells and plates were scattered around a small bench near the back. A vintage stereo sat propped up on a wood laminate wall shelf with two huge speakers on either side, right next to a four section small window strewn with cobwebs. Footballs, soccer balls, water guns, golf clubs, baseball bats, and toys filled bins around the perimeter, carefully organized as not to impede the path of the snowblower and lawn mower. A clear area in the center of the garage was just big enough for four chairs to be spaced comfortably apart with a bright shop light hanging directly overhead.

After we had made it inside, I carefully brought the noisy door to the ground and felt my stomach swell with excitement. I gathered four plastic deck chairs and arranged them in a square formation. We sat down, and Heub, Bo, and I watched Slater intently as he pulled out a mason jar from his bag and began breaking pieces off of a small Christmas tree nug of a strain known as "Thai Fusion." A piney diesel aroma filled the garage, raising my desire to taste this fabled plant.

Once Slater had prepared the bubbler, he stood up and walked over to me, holding the piece out. As I reached out to take it, he said; "Just put your thumb over the carb hole here, and don't blow into it. I'll light it for you."

I brought the stem to my mouth and began to inhale as the lighter licked the bowl. Harsh smoke burned my lungs as Slater took it away, and an overwhelming feeling of novelty danced around in my mind. I had never inhaled anything like this before, and my fresh lungs recoiled at the hot tar that was being pulled into them. I exhaled the smoke and coughed a few times with a searing feeling in my throat. After seventeen years, I finally understood what smoking felt like, and I wondered how much worse cigarettes were.

Instantly following this hit, I felt light headed and the sensation of a small seed being planted that would grow very quickly. I rested back into my chair and watched as Bo and Slater naturally blew out smoke from the green and purple glass bubbler. Time sailed by and then I noticed Slater handing the vaporizer to me, and saw no reason to pass on another hit. I took a deep inhale, and exhaled like I was trying to see my breath on a winter day. I noted a difference in my lungs compared to the smoke, and let the succulent vapor drift off my tongue. I passed the piece left to Bo and watched a haze rest in the closed garage atmosphere as the four of us burnt and exhaled spicy fumes. I only had a brief moment of contemplation before Slater was handing me yet another packed bubbler, and again I saw no reason to turn it down. I loved the sensory stimulation and act of smoking thus far, even though the effects were only beginning. Happy to consume as much as available, I wondered about the so called "addictive properties" of weed as I carefully held the bubbler in my hand. I lit it myself this time, and prepared for the hot smoke to fill my lungs.

Following another large hit and forceful exhale, I quickly handed the bubbler back to Slater, and began to feel an ever growing euphoria and spaciness. I felt so far out of my head, unconcerned with responsibilities, school, sports, health, and family. I was focused only on that exact moment of pure wonder at this great new experience before me; sitting in the garage with three of my childhood friends, smoking weed and having a great time just for the sake of fun. I was not worried about being caught, or what these guys were thinking of me. I only felt love, and as if my mind were floating up through the clouds, headed towards space.

My focus on the experience was diverted when Bo asked me, "So, what do you think?"

Slater chimed in as well: "Yeah, do you like smoking weed?"

I looked at Heub who said, "It's different."

Without thinking much about how I would sound or be received, I drawled "Why can't we be like this all the time?" causing Slater to laugh and an interesting expression to appear on the faces of Bo and Heub. I had uttered what the stereotypical pothead would say after they smoked for the first time, and I believe that everyone knew in this moment that much consumption was in the future. The era of me refusing to smoke was over, and now I could come along for my friends high adventures, hoping to catch up on the fun.

Shortly after the smoke session had begun, Heub's phone rang. It was his father, demanding he come home. He pushed back to no avail, and soon Heub was opening the garage door, ready to make the journey back across town. We said our farewells to him, briefly reveling in the fun evening. Slater and Bo encouraged him to avoid direct confrontation with his conservative parents, lest his activities this evening be revealed. The garage felt a bit empty once he had left, and the three of us knew that the night would soon be coming to a close. We had to enjoy the remainder of our time together before going to bed, and starting another day of school.

I directed my attention toward Slater, pondering his excessive consumption of marijuana over the past years, and began to develop an understanding of his habit. I was staring at his face when I began to notice the edges become very clear with a magnification effect. This visual effect intensified, and I started giggling as I watched Slater become increasingly more 3d. I attempted to describe to him how "real" he looked, and how his face was moving towards me. He laughed and said: "This dude is high as fuck."

    I was entertained by my experience and could not contain laughter as I looked towards Bo who appeared to be high, but not as high as I was. These visual effects were very unique and I did not expect them from cannabis. I wanted so badly to describe to my friends what it was like, but remained unsatisfied with my description and lack of fitting words. Brief dialogue was traded between Slater and Bo as I began staring intently at a bolt on the garage door. My thoughts were compounding with peculiar ideas about this hardware and its unique position on the door. The bolt began to magnify, and I thought about how it looked almost like an island in a sea of white, and though I was entirely immersed in this experience, my captivation at this tiny piece of metal amused me. I could not understand how I was having so many creative and euphoric thoughts while staring at something so simple and mundane.

    Breaking my trance, Slater told me that it was time for him to head home. I noticed all of his things had been packed, and that Bo was already standing. The three of us left the garage, and I said a brief and unceremonious farewell to my buddies. Slater hopped in Bo's silver and teal 1995 F-150, and then they were off into the night. From full company to solitude, the swift end of the evening weighed on me. I brushed my teeth and went straight to bed, just escaping my compounding thoughts and confusing emotions.

I slept well that night and treated the next day like any other day of school. My life had changed because of that night, but I did not yet realize it. I was just a teenager having fun with my friends. I felt normal, waking up sober and going about my responsibilities. Hundreds more smoke sessions awaited me in the coming years, but little did I know that this night would hold such sentiment for me. I did not realize then how much nostalgia I would attach to this first time I smoked, and how strongly I would desire to go back.

This particular night began a story with me and three of my childhood friends. We had grown together over the past years, and had shared the celebration of Slater's transition to adulthood by getting high in my garage. It was simple and beautiful, but fleeting in nature. Had I known what fate held in store for each of us, I would have relished those moments all the more dearly. Had I known how our friendships would change, I would have written every detail about that night.

Instead, there are many things about this time that I will never know. Questions I never asked my friends, and feelings that are lost to the past. Perhaps this is why many people say that high school years are the best years of your life because there is so much that is unknown. You are thrown into an environment with people who will soon disperse in different directions, but you are not aware of how soon many of those people will disappear from your life. Your focus may be on sports, academics, social relations, extracurriculars, or delinquency, but the fact of the matter is that your perspective is not all encompassing. There are inevitable shortcomings of understanding because your brain is not fully maturated, and as such there is much mystery. For this reason, a rose tinted lens over the past may develop as our minds fill in the blanks of our experiences. What once may have been an uncomfortable or unenjoyable experience transforms into a positive reminiscence.

Despite any explanation for these feelings, the fact of the matter is that this time is forever gone. I like to think that the creator and universe keep a record of everything, but never in my life will I again feel moments exactly like those. Weed would never be like this again because the circumstances would never be the same again. As quickly as the night began, it ended. Only four people carry the foggy memory of that night, and each one of us holds a uniquely irreplicable experience of it.

Chapter 5

The Rabbit Hole

Very soon after my first cannabis experience, I had the opportunity to take magic mushrooms with Slater. I had smoked weed no more than five times before I had the option of ramping things up a bit and delving deeper into the psychedelic world. Now that I had tried an entheogenic plant and tasted a new consciousness, I was hungry for more. Marijuana, being hallucinogenic in its own way, is considered by many to be far less mind bending and psychologically dangerous than traditional psychedelics. I had done extensive research on the potential consequences of hallucinogen use and had discovered that from a purely physiological standpoint, they were safer than sugar and coffee. Psychologically, however, they could not compare to anything I had experienced. Further exploration had been on my mind for months now, though I did not believe that I would find the source or opportunity.

Then, Slater's dealer, who moved lots of drugs, including Xanax, marijuana, acid, and opiates, told him one day that he had mushrooms. Slater jumped at the opportunity and bought an ounce, sharing his first experience with Lewis. They described it as groovy, and all I could think of was lying in a dimly lit room watching a deep blue colored wall breathe with green swirls. Maybe even peering out the window of a 60s hippie van into space while listening to wide music-that's what groovy was to me.

I was not particularly afraid or anxious; instead my curiosity was overflowing, and I was incredibly excited to experience my first-ever psychedelic trip. I had spent many nights reading people's description of their experiences on Erowid, and watching Youtubers emotionally detail their passes through these peculiar realms. I had a particular egotism surrounding my understanding, and felt more equipped to handle a trip than my friends who had done little to no research of their own. Despite having been vehemently against drug use in the few months prior, I was now a well-studied student, and I sought the introspective and teaching aspect of these substances. I did not desire a purely euphoric trip. Rather, I wanted to dip my toe into the shamanic world. I wanted to understand and feel what others had felt, dispel the clichés perpetuated by culture, and touch the spiritual traditions that emerged from the Mesoamerican temples and religions throughout the world

The night began as Slater and I sat in the living room of my childhood house on a school night. Our plans were already in place, and I had come to terms with the fact that I was about to take a new drug for the very first time. Holding a mason jar full of beige stems streaked with blue, Slater looked at me and asked, "So, how much do you want to take? A gram? Two?"

"Two seems like too much. Let me start with one, and if I don't feel it I can take more," I answered.

"No, dude, that's not how you're supposed to take them. Why don't you just take 1.5?"

I paused for a moment, and figured Slater was right. That was a good starting place. It was strong enough that I could get a sufficient sense of the psychedelic waves, but it was still in the shallow waters in case I got knocked over.

"1.5 is good."

Slater spun the lid off the mason jar and stuck his pale white nose into it, inhaling deeply.

"Ahh, boomers!"

He then pulled a scale out of his black backpack and carefully weighed out 1.5 grams of thickly stemmed mushrooms with wilted brown caps.

"Alrighty, there you go, buddy. Magic mushrooms."

He motioned me over and dumped the contents of the scale into my hands. I looked down at what had been given to me. Never before had I seen or touched this particular thing, yet it had been used for thousands of years by humans around the world. Incredible punishments were in place for those found to be using such a treacherous thing; yet there I was, looking down at what appeared to be harmless little pieces of fungi. I wondered what secret room of some mycological drug dealer's house they had been cultivated in, and how the growing process had played out. Whether they came from miles away off the deep web, or from down the street in an unsuspecting civilian house, their final destination was my hands.

"Ready to take them?" Slater asked, interrupting my daydream. I noticed he had weighed out another portion on the scale for himself.

"Yeah, how much are you taking?"

"Point seven five. I'm just looking to get a little buzz tonight. I ain't goin' as deep as you."

With that, the two of us began eating the mushrooms. They tasted strange. I had heard that chewing them for longer made the trip come on faster, so I kept the wet and mushy pile of earthy matter floating around in my mouth. While doing this, I sat in a wheelie office chair, rocking myself back and forth, and looking at a set of shelves embedded into the wall. Family pictures were carefully placed on the shelves next to small mirrors, a marble egg and apple, and a glass ball with air bubbles suspended in it. Next to them was an arched doorway with a rectangular clay artwork depicting a rose bouquet over top of it. Its neutral beige color blended in seamlessly with the color of the walls, and though I knew it had certainly been there for years, I wondered why it had been so long since I had taken note of it. I felt a bubbling excitement at what visual effects were possible, and played with ideas of the ways these objects could be morphed and changed.

My train of accelerating thoughts was interrupted by my mother.

"Will you guys take Mika for a walk?"

A walk! What an excellent idea for the come-up and I answered with a nod. I wrangled the dog and headed out onto the driveway with Slater. We took a half hour-trot around the block which was incredibly peaceful. It was hazy though—I could not remember anything notable happening on that walk, just the calming sensation of moving my legs around a very familiar neighborhood. I had few preoccupations: no concerns about school, fears of violence, or worries about family or friends. It was a beautifully simple Tuesday night, and I was a kid excited to experience something powerful and outside of the ordinary. If I could go back and dawdle in those particular moments of wonder and ignorance, in the headspace of that time with heartfelt excitement and extensive unknowing, I would savor and describe every aspect of it.

Once Slater and I made it back to the driveway, I let Mika off her leash and watched her bound up the driveway, tail wagging. The night air was cool and crisp, and as I walked up the steps of the porch, I realized that my experience was just on the horizon. I opened the door and stepped into a thick warmth that caused a heavy sensation to grow in my body. Slater followed close behind me, remarking on how the effects had begun to set in. I shut the door behind and looked around the living room, expecting some kind of visual effect to begin. Nothing appeared out of the ordinary besides the fact that the room seemed ever-so-slightly larger. Maybe even a little foreign, like my first day in the sixth grade classroom.

Slater sauntered over to the couch and relaxed back into the soft brown leather cushion. He had an aura of teenage carelessness and calm, and I felt at ease around him. I was not at all concerned about what he was thinking of me, or about any unspoken emotions or desires of his. His state of mind was unfiltered, and I trusted him to be a good trip sitter. I knew some kind of effect was starting, so I found the desk chair I had sat in earlier and rested back into it. This caused a sensation of blood and lucidity to dribble towards the back of my brain, leaving the front feeling light and floaty. This euphoric feeling seemed to linger and grow slowly.

I was happy that I was in it. Mushrooms felt good, and though I knew I had just started the come-up, I sensed deeper things would be revealed in time. I tried to remain as conscious as possible of what was happening. I was convinced that this trip held something very special for me, and that I would need to recall it and reflect on it for some kind of greater development. Unfortunately this ended up having the inverse effect of what I intended. Instead of full immersion in the present moment, I was preoccupied with what would come next.

My thought stream was broken by Slater inquiring about my experience. I took a moment to respond and said, "I really like mushrooms."

"Hell yeah, dude, Brady got some really good ones. I'm gonna hit him up and see if I can get more."

Even more mushrooms: glorious! I did not know anyone else who had them available for sale, and with the positivity of this experience so far, I was ecstatic that more could be on the way. Drug deals were sketchy, but I was out of harm's way with Slater assuming responsibility. He was the one getting in the car, trading the cash, and walking out with the contraband. I got to reap the rewards which seemed selfish at times, but my involvement did not change what Slater was going to do. I did not judge his insatiable desire for psychoactives, and though I voiced my concerns, he relentlessly pursued a path of intoxication. My home and I were safe and could be a source of support for Slater in a time of difficulty. But now we were just friends having fun, finding our way.

Not long after I had sat down, the visual effects began to manifest. I first noticed that the entire living room had a pink hue to it, almost like neon gas was seeping out from the walls. Then, I observed the soft yellow light from the lamp on the desk create an ambient gradient of shading that stretched down the walls. This combined with the velvety darkness of the night pouring in through the windows to form patches of contrast and shadow that seemed to amplify the surfaces they rested on. The effect was far more mild than what I had expected, but it was novel nonetheless.

I noticed that the curtains draped across the front window displayed some unique patterns-rows of softball sized mandalas-and the longer I stared at them, the more

I began to notice movement. I thought that the curtains were swaying slightly from the air being blown out of the register, but then I noticed the shapes turn in a clockwise direction. I could not decide why this curtain was behaving the way it was, even though I knew I was experiencing some level of visual alteration. As the pink mist appeared to stain the curtain, my curiosity got the best of me, and I had to know if it was truly moving.

Eyes locked on the anomaly, I got up out of the desk chair and walked over to the curtain.

"What's up?" Slater asked. "Do you see someone outside?"

"This curtain looks like it's moving, dude."

I took a bit of the fabric in my hand, rubbing it between my fingers. The texture felt like a grid, and I inspected it more closely to find that there was no movement. I half expected to see a tiny colony of creatures as the cause of the movement, but it was simply a curtain. Slightly disappointed, I walked over to my chair, and noticed Slater watch me the entire way.

"You're starting to trip now, aren't you?" Slater laughed.

"No man, it was really moving! Look at it!"

The two of us stared at the curtain and watched as a draft caused a slight vibration through it."

"Oh yeah, I can see where that would trip you out."

"It's weird, man, the circles on it look like they're kind of moving too, independent of the sway. They almost look like clocks."

"Really? That's sweet."

I turned my attention away from the curtain and noticed that the rotating circles had moved away from it and were now across my entire vision.

"Woah, I see a bunch of spirals now!"

"What!" Slater snickered.

Translucent circular vortexes patterned in a grid across my sight, similar to the visual effect one gets after staring at a light for too long. I soaked in this moment, thoroughly enjoying it, until I decided to close my eyes. Immediate blackness was followed by the slow emergence of one large spinning vortex of black and white. I was reminded of the time I stared at an optical illusion video with a very similar object, a black and white swirling whirlwind.

I could not decide why this particular distortion had manifested itself, and I wondered if it held some kind of hidden message. This was one of the most stereotypical images associated with so-called "trippy" artwork, and I was having a very clear exposure to it. Wonder dominated my mind as I tried to keep the image in my visual field, but slowly it began to dissolve. I opened my eyes to a slightly hazy room that had smooth edges and a mild boost in saturation. I was enamored by what I was experiencing and I wanted to know how much longer I could enjoy it.

"How long has it been?" I asked.

Slater looked down at his watch, and then back up at me.

"About an hour and half."

How great, the peak was coming on and I had another two hours or so of powerful experience. I was excited to float into the coming levels of the trip and even had a journal on the desk to write down any revelations that would come to me. Then, I heard a knock on the door and a sense of dread dropped in my stomach. Who in the heck was here? I got up out of my chair to peek through the blinds, and as I was walking over, Slater said, "I invited Sara."

I stopped in my tracks and glared at him in silence.

"Why, dude?" I whispered venomously.

"I was going to tell you. I thought you would be okay with it."

Unbelievable. Here I was about to peak on my first-ever psychedelic experience and my friend decided to invite over a girl who I was neither expecting nor comfortable around. I wanted badly to send Slater and her off on their own, but feared how this hostile action would affect my trip. I knew that the longer I waited to open the door, the more awkward it was going to be, so I pulled it open. Sure enough, there was Sara smiling up at me with curly dark brown hair that stretched down to her elbows. Her skin was caked white with accents of pink at her cheekbones. She had dark eyebrows and eyeliner juxtapositioned with blue eyes. I must have had a detached look of frustration and apathy, but it was evident that she was excited to see me.

"Hey, man."

"Hey." I murmured. Then I heard Slater shout, "Sara! Get in here!"

I looked into the house, and then back at Sara, making eye contact with her for a moment. There seemed to be an understanding that I was neither excited to see her nor aware of her invitation. I knew it would be awkward to turn her away, and so I invited her in. She walked into the living room and, after exchanging some excited greetings with Slater, joined him on the couch. Irritated, I returned to my desk chair, and did my best to ignore them

"We're both tripping on 'shrooms right now. He took a gram and a half," Slater bragged.

"Oh dude, awesome! What's it like, Christian?" she asked.

Uneager to waste my breath trying to explain what I was feeling, I said "It's pretty cool. I was seeing swirls in the room earlier."

Sara faked a giggle and had her attention drawn back by Slater. I hoped that they would entertain each other so that I could immerse myself in the trip and focus on the peak. Unfortunately, Sara wanted to join in on the fun, and Slater suggested they take a few rips out of the bong. He boasted about the great privilege my mother had extended to us-a safe place to get high-oversharing the fact that she smoked weed too. He built up a hype around it, and due to my intoxicated state and peer pressure, I reluctantly said it was okay.

Slater then pulled a big jar of weed out of his bag and asked me to go grab the bong. Frustrated, and figuring once they had weed they would stop being a nuisance, I fumbled my way into my bedroom and found the green glass piece. I carried it back into the living room and passed it to Slater before falling into my chair in a huff. Sara's eyes widened as he packed up the bowl which sent waves of irritation through my bones. I leaned back and looked up at the ceiling, trying to drown out their voices before the sound of a lighter and bubbling water caused me to redirect my gaze to the couch. Sara was batting at a thin cloud of smoke hanging in the middle of the room while Slater tried to regain his composure.

"Ready to take a hit? It's packed up," Slater said, holding the bong out in front of Sara.

Once again, her eyes widened, and an excited smile grew across her face.

"You're sure your mom's okay with this?" she asked, looking at me.

"She totally is! I bet she would come out here and smoke with us. Lynne, get out here and take a rip!" Slater shouted. There was no response from my mother's bedroom, and I was taken aback at Slater's insolence and disregard for boundaries. Here he was in my house, asserting what my mom was okay with and yelling at her to come smoke weed. Had I not been bathing in the psychedelic pool, I would have been able to express some clear boundaries. I shut my eyes and shook my head before opening them back up and seeing Sara take a big rip off the bong. She cleared all of the smoke and, after choking it out, coughed loudly for what seemed like hours. They both hooted about the size of the rip and laughed boisterously.

Then, from the other room, I heard my mom say, "Christian," in a punitive tone and felt a knot of dread manifest in me. I knew it had to do with Sara and Slater, and as I got up to deal with the consequences, I returned their looks of concern with a glare. I walked out of the living room, taking a right past my bedroom and to the end of the hallway where my mom's door was shut. I took a deep breath and walked into the room where she was sitting with a pink-faced scowl.

"Who's out there coughing so loud?" she asked.

"It's Sara. Slater invited her over without telling me."

"You need to tell her she can't be doing that here. If her parents find out about it, I'll be in so much trouble!" she insisted.

"I'm sorry, I thought it would be okay," I said sheepishly, turning away to head back to the living room.

"Dude, think before you let people come over here and start smoking down. Just because I said you and Slater can doesn't mean I want the whole neighborhood to know!"

"I'm sorry, I should have told them no. What do you want me to do?"

"Go out there and tell them to stop!" she said, directing her attention from me back to a book she was holding. Immense guilt and embarrassment welled up in me, paired with a growing feeling of nakedness and vulnerability. I looked down at the ground, and apologized once more with no response. I left her room and shut the door behind me, noting how terrible it was that I had to deal with this right in the middle of my trip. It was all Slater's fault too.

I returned to the living room where Slater and Sara were in the middle of a private conversation. It took them a minute to notice me before Slater said, "What's going on? Is she coming out to smoke?"

"No, she doesn't want us to smoke anymore," I spat back. I could not believe how out of touch he was about what was happening.

"What? Why not? Tell her to get out here and take a rip!" Slater insisted.

"No! Put the weed away and give me the bong." I walked over to the couch where the two of them were sitting. Slater stared at me for a moment and then frowned. I remained next to the couch in silence before Slater laughed and said, "Fine, I bet she will next time. Here." I took the bong and carried it out of the living room, looking feverishly for a place to hide it. I wanted to make sure neither my mom nor Slater would find it, so I hid it under the kitchen sink behind all of the bottles of cleaner and soap. Satisfied with the spot, I walked back into the living room and flopped into the office chair, rolling across the floor.

I took a deep breath and felt a sense of relief as I exhaled; the weed was put away, and my company were entertaining themselves. With the external problems solved, I felt myself sliding back into the trip and returning to the strange feeling of euphoria and warped thoughts. I knew the peak was coming on soon, so after pulling out my ipod touch and headphones, I announced "I'm peaking, I'm gonna listen to some music."

"Right on, man," Slater said, preoccupied with Sara. I put on the song "DMT" by XXYYXX and leaned back into my chair, shutting my eyes. Immediately, I saw a two dimensional grid of green lines against the void span out in front of me and evolve into a three dimensional structure. It appeared as a sort of matrix, and I felt great curiosity and astonishment at the hallucination. The power and intensity of my thoughts grew, as meaningful internal dialogue and phrases seemed to come out of nowhere. A feeling of divine understanding swept over me as I tried helplessly to write down what I was feeling. The letters came out large and the words did not represent my thoughts. My questions were answered, but I could not remember what they were, only their resolution. My desire to record my thoughts and feelings was deep, but I could neither describe nor frame the experience I was having.

The magnitude of my experience continued to grow, and I began evaluating my life choices critically. I felt proud of my decisions: choosing healthy eating, an active lifestyle, and obedience to my mother. I realized I had a lack of mental organization, that I had not been exercising enough control over my mind, and that I had been attaching myself to emotions and letting them guide me. I understood that I had drawn conclusions based upon personal biases for the sake of my own psyche. I recognized the fragility of my mind, and how sensitive a person I was.

Sheer amazement at my feelings lingered as I felt my soul separate from my body. I became convinced that my consciousness and thoughts now were starkly different than in my regular life and that my perspective existed on a spectrum. I saw consciousness as a series of levels: conditioning from birth and the subjective sense of self, tiered realizations from meditation and psychedelics, all the way up to enlightenment. The music twisted in my ears and resonated through my mind as I seemed to have no control over what I was thinking and being spoken to by my higher self. A melting feeling trickled down from the top of the left side of my head, and gave me the odd sensation that the right side of my face was composed of a different material than the left..

Pure clarity washed over me as I found the peak. I was ascended, I could see that existence was simply a game that my spirit was playing through a bodily vessel. I knew I was not at the top of the psychedelic mountain, but high up on it, and tasting what I had so deeply craved. This feeling faded almost as quickly as it came and I tried so hard to hold onto it. I recognized that I was coming down and began writing furiously, trying to put into words everything I had just seen and felt

Then I paused, cold. A soothing awareness swept over me as I understood that witnessing it was all that was needed. There did not need to be an explanation; the experience was whole in and of itself. Though my desire was to define my feelings, words did that very feeling an injustice. I was happy with my realization that life was a collection of comedic things that spiritual beings were playing in. I figured it was not always our place to use language to explain phenomenon, and that many things are better left as raw experience.

My stability grew as my perception shrank, and eventually I felt capable of coming back to my environment.

With a mollified whisper, I said "wow" and took off my headphones, feeling like I had been washed in cosmic water. I stared at my journal with a smile, and then at my friends. The peak was gone, and I had no meaningful writing to show for it. All my questions had been answered and were now within me, yet I had written no coherent sentences in my journal.

"Welcome back," Slater said "How was the peak?"

"Yeah, man, tell us about it." Sara said.

"It was amazing! I love mushrooms. I came close to enlightenment," I explained warmly.

"Hell yes, dude, aren't they great? I have to get some more from Brady."

"What was enlightenment like?" Sara asked.

I furrowed my brow, looking away, and then back at them. "That's kind of what I realized; you can't really put it into words. It's like a feeling."

"Aww come on, man, you gotta have more than that!" Sara persisted. "What did you write?" I looked at my journal and the few distorted words I had written. The letters were a mixture of large and wobbly to small and neat. Incomplete sentences and ideas were scattered about the page. The only comprehensible phrase was "All of life is meaning."

"The only thing I wrote that makes any sense is All of life is meaning."

"Huh? That can't be. You were writing like the whole time. Let me see," Sara asked.

I did not want to reveal how ridiculous the writing was, so I shut the book and said, "That's all there is. This is my creative writing journal, too. I wonder if I should take the page out before I turn it in for my next assignment."

"Leave it in there; I bet Mr. Toowin would like to see it," Slater joked.

"The best way I can describe it is, it's a lot to take in, but it's overwhelmingly beautiful."

"I guess so," Sara said, dissatisfied.

The night rolled on peacefully for another hour during the come down before Slater and Sara left. Even though their company had been undesirable for a time, I felt a lot of warmth and love towards them at the end. I was glad they had been there for the experience and that I had some curious people to talk about it with. The night had gone well, all things considered, and I felt a greater sense of friendship with both of them for accompanying me in this experience.

Once they were gone, I felt guilty for losing my temper. I knew neither of them would take it personally though, and so I left things as they were. Then I readied my things for the next day and got in bed, blissfully relaxed. I laid there for a while, just enjoying the feeling of calm before slowly drifting off to sleep and awaking comfortably the next day. I had to be at school for a morning lifting session, and after hinting to a teammate a year behind me about my actions the night before, I felt a great deal of functionality. Here I was, enjoying the day, going through the motions of being a student after sailing through a psychedelic plain less than 12 hours before. A little lost in thought, but incredibly smiley, I enjoyed my day. I found great novelty in the mundane-like I was rediscovering and experiencing some of the parts of being human.

Some lingering effects outside of the spaciness and novelty remained in the following days. I had a greater need to be in nature, and took more walks home from school through the woods. I also had lost my desire to smoke weed and figured it was related to the fact that I had wanted something more powerful from the beginning. The few times I had smoked weed prior to this experience, I almost always left feeling a bit underwhelmed and craving something more. The mushrooms had temporarily satiated that desire, but I still felt I was only wading in the shallow end of the pool.

Surely, my experience with mushrooms opened more doors and questions than it answered. It took me over a year of reflection to unpack and understand it fully, but I never bought into the critics' assertions pertaining to the triviality of psychedelics. This first experience gave me such a profound sense of peace and real experience that no one could convince me was false or unmeaningful. Still, I invited judgment by sharing my experience. Whether it was from friends and family, strangers on the internet, or hyper criticism of my own ideologies, to this day I carry a gem with me from each of my psychedelic experiences. My habitual cannabis use was another area that only served as ammunition against my claims, from self and others, yet the majesty continues to endure in my sobriety.

Chapter 6

Senior Prank

One Sunday around midnight in late May, Heub, Bo and I were sitting a few hundred feet outside of our high school boundary in a beige 2001 Toyota Corolla. Our plan was to latch the gate with some bike locks and cause mayhem for traffic in the morning. We had to do something; ever since middle school, we had talked about a legendary senior prank, and those who came before us set the bar very high. Our freshmen year, the senior class had managed to pile all the desks and chairs in a giant bundle in the middle of each classroom. There had even been rumors of desks ending up on the roof, pigs let loose, and a giant chicken statue being strung up for all to see. It was a great way to go out-letting the entire school know that you were powerful graduates who had transcended the bonds of high school.

Unfortunately, after the prank freshmen year where someone broke their collarbone and lost a sports scholarship, the administration asserted a zero-tolerance policy. They said anyone who was caught would not be walking at graduation and would have their diploma withheld. So, basically every senior that we knew with a shred of self preservation stayed away from the fabled end-of-the-year prank, except us. We really had been trying to think of something as our last days here crept up on us, and kicked ourselves for not doing it earlier. It was a fact; we were too late to pull off anything good. The time to prank was a couple weeks ago before the window for typical senior shenanigans.

Now, the school was expecting a prank and this was very obvious during our stakeout. The driveway into the back of the school had an unusual amount of activity for a Sunday at midnight, and a figure with a flashlight would periodically jump out of a car and search around before making the rounds again. Heub was not having it.

"This isn't normal, guys; they are expecting us. Let's do it another night," he whispered.

"Heub, we got the locks already. We are doing this," Bo asserted.

"We can do better with more time and planning. Don't you think so, Christian?"

"We're already here, why not just do it? I can't really think of anything else to do."

"Let's just go back to your place and call it a night. We can figure out something better and do it another time this week."

"No, Heub! We've been trying to think of something for months. You know they are going to be patrolling every night. We just gotta run up and lock the gate. It's easy." Bo assured him

"We gotta lock all the gates, Bo. Plus, they probably have bolt cutters to just take them off. I'm telling you guys, we gotta do something better."

I watched from the driver's seat while my two friends bantered and began to wonder if there ever would be another opportunity. We were already so close to the end of school, and so close to the prank, why not just go through with it? Otherwise, I feared nothing would ever happen, and we all would live with the regret of never trying.

"Let's just do it. If anything happens, we all take off different directions. Where should we meet?" I said with hesitation.

"We can't meet back at the car." Heub answered.

"How about under the bridge?" Bo offered.

"That's a plan. Let's go." I opened the door into the crisp night air and stepped out onto the beaten road. A special chill crept up my spine as I hopped onto the grassy curb with my two buddies. My solar plexus seared and a nervousness pooled in my stomach. This was the sweet adrenaline of doing something I was not supposed to with high risk and high reward. I loved it, but not everything I did with my body was entirely by choice. I was in the absolute present moment, for I could not afford to miss any detail, lest I suffer because of it. The three of us knew how to depend on our instincts here, as our years of teepeeing, dumping doughnuts on cars, and trespassing created great awareness of these sorts of environments.

We hurried towards the first gate on the back parking lot of the school, and Bo quickly cinched on the bike lock. His eyes were wide, and there was obvious doubt in his mind. This was uncharacteristic; I expected him to be, though cautious, spearheading the mission. Heub and I both had a lock, and now we would have to make it over to the front of the school where the other two gates were. To get there, we would have to stay towards the edge of a large, exposed parking lot where a grassy mound was dotted with thick pine trees for cover.

When we were about 100 feet from the sidewalk and starting our journey along the ridge, a pair of headlights shot up out of a hill on the edge of the school lot. The scraping sound of high RPMs and rubber pushing gravel told me someone was coming fast, right in our direction.

I immediately crouched down until I was lying prone on the ground, and then pushed myself back as close to the brush as possible. A big concrete wall behind the treeline was blocking my escape, so I tried to blend as well as I could by keeping a low profile. I looked right to make sure my friends were hidden as well, and noticed them both hunkered down on one knee. I watched anxiously as the car got closer before the sound of footsteps clipping across the asphalt caught my ear. I glanced back and saw my two friends sprinting towards the gate.

I got up onto my hands and knees, tensing my body and preparing to make a run for it, but it was too late. The car was already too close, and my friends had abandoned me without any warning. Now security was heading right for the gate to investigate the perimeter, blocking my only way out. In the distance, I heard Bo shouting, "Heub, wait up! Heub!" and I knew for sure they were long gone.

The headlights of the car were burning straight at me, so I pulled my hood up and squished my face and body down into the grass. Everything was bright for a few seconds until the lights were off me. I peeked up and noticed that the car was now at the gate, pointing its lights out towards the sidewalk. Then I heard a door open and watched a shadowy figure wielding a flashlight step out into the night, not 50 feet from me. The door slammed, and I heard footsteps crunch gravel as the person walked towards the gate, aiming the flashlight directly at the lock. He may have heard Bo's shouts, or caught a glimpse of the two of them running away as he was now preoccupied with investigating beyond the gate. I figured this was my only chance. I shot up from my position and ran full bore along the concrete wall.

I smashed through low hanging pine branches while sprinting as fast as I could towards the opposite end of the parking lot. Through a dozen trees, I ran like a bull before stealing a glance back and saw the person now standing right where I had been laying, aiming the light down the line of trees. The beam bounced and seemed to be growing brighter, so I continued sprinting through the line of trees until I emerged onto the exposed edge of the ridge with one tall poplar tree looking over the parking lot. I stopped and squatted down, quickly assessing the environment. Between me and the public road was another big parking lot. On one side, the school football stadium, the other, an open stretch of bus parking along the front of the school. There, just a few hundred feet from me by the stadium, a red sedan was parked a short ways from a figure chaining up the gates.

    I dropped down as low as I could and crawled back into the ridge, keeping a close eye on the man who I figured to be security. He tested the gate once and then got back into his car before coasting off towards the front of the school. Then the car halted. I clenched my teeth and held my breath. Had I been seen? That other guy is probably texting him about trespassers. My spot had very little cover, and I could be crept up on at any second.

    I watched impatiently while the red car idled for 30 long seconds before easing off again. I took the opportunity and sprinted towards the stadium where a large brick ticket booth offered cover.

    I crouched behind the booth, putting it between me and the place I just been. The only thing here was the locked up football field. For a brief second, I remembered the faces of parents in this very booth who had sold me tickets a few months prior. If only they could see me now. I scanned the open parking lot looking for any signs of security, and realized that this was the home stretch. One hundred fifty feet of asphalt stood between me and freedom. I crouched back down and took a moment to catch my breath before peering around the booth one last time to check that the coast was clear. Standing right where I had been laying only seconds ago was the man with the flashlight, and so now was the time. I hauled as fast as I could towards the road through the exposed and well lit parking lot, seeming to pound my legs across the hard ground without any conscious thought. Then I was bounding over the sidewalk on the opposite end of the road before I slowed down to find the overgrown path over the guardrail into the woods. Heub and Bo were 50 feet in; we made it.

Chapter 7

LSD

The first encounter I had with LSD was during my sophomore year of high school when Louis and Slater took a sub-100ug dose. My only prior knowledge of this drug was a story of my god-brother taking it and having an absolute psychotic break where the police got involved. This was the "hardest" drug my friends had ever taken, and besides knowing that it was illegal, I had heard myths about loss of sanity and irreparable damage as a result of taking it. Despite this, being in the company of the two trippers was not particularly upsetting to me. I knew nothing of the specific effects of this drug, and the only funky thing that happened was Slater putting on a dog collar, and marching around on all fours in a grassy field. At that time, I never considered what it would be like to take this drug, or how long I would spend researching it. This experience was the only exposure I had to LSD before jumping down the rabbit hole years later in search of what it was all about.

A common occurrence that happened frequently throughout my psychedelic exploration was substances becoming available at incredibly opportune times. It was not about seeking them, rather them finding their way to me. Some may label this as sheer coincidence, while others may play it as a part of the connected universe, but the facts of the situation remain. I was at Wilx park after graduation with one of my childhood friends, Tor. The fall day was gray with a light drizzle, and the two of us had come to the park looking for some people to chat and smoke with. I knew that drugs of all kinds were traded and consumed around this park, but today's venture was about to be written as too dreary for the hippies to come out of their houses. Then I heard wet tires on pavement and turned to see a 90's sedan careening down the road, coming to an abrupt stop next to the curb where we were standing. The driver side door opened, and a tall individual with spiky, banana yellow hair who we both recognized jumped out: Duke.

"Hey, what are you guys doing here?" he asked with a surprised look, as he walked towards us

"We were looking for some people to smoke with." Tor answered.

"I'm down. How's it going, buddy?" Duke affectionately asked as he and Tor hugged.

"It's going good, man. I haven't seen you since high school."

"Yeah, life's been crazy; I don't have much time today, but let's share a bowl."

Tor pulled a glass pipe out of his pocket, and they both threw in some bud.

"By the way, are you guys trying to buy some acid?"

I could not believe it; yes, that's exactly what I was

trying to do. I even had some cash on me just in case the opportunity arose. Tor looked at me and Duke followed his gaze. I tried to contain my excitement and said: " I've been looking for some."

"Good deal, I got a whole sheet in the car. I'm on some right now, and it's really good. Double dipped too. How much do you want to buy?"

I had been warned of dangerous research chemicals and fakes being sold in place of LSD, and I figured buying from a friend who had taken it was the safest bet. I only had enough money to buy a single tab, but I was curious about his prices.

"How much for one?" I asked.

"Just ten."

"How much for ten?"

He paused for a moment and then followed with, "I can do 10 for 80."

"Yeah, I'll buy some."

Duke slipped his hand into his back pocket and pulled out a tinfoil square and tweezers. He hunkered over the tabs as he unfolded the foil to show me a ten-strip, and then handed it my direction. I held out a ten dollar bill, which made him bring the tabs back close to his torso, and break off a single with his tweezers. I hoped he had not thought I was trying to scam him or take advantage of his intoxicated state; I just wanted one tab. Once the deal was done, I looked him in the eyes and smiled.

"Have fun with that," he grinned.

"Ready to smoke?" Tor interrupted.

"Let's do it."

The three of us proceeded to hit a few bowls, entirely unafraid of any legal consequences of our actions. I can only imagine what would have happened had a cop rolled up at that time. Not only were we smoking weed, but also fresh off a drug deal with a schedule one substance. We were all intoxicated and planning to drive home, especially Duke; what a trip.

After saying our farewells and wishing the best for each other, we parted ways into the evening. I played with the novelty of this coincidence all the way up until the trip, concluding it had to be a part of the big picture.

•••

Over a month later, I decided that I was ready to take the tab. I had taken a week off of smoking marjuana to prepare myself for this experience, and I was also accompanied by a longtime childhood friend, Dakota. He was going to be trip sitting me, and with plans to see the sunrise the following day, we went to bed early. After waking up around 6am, we had breakfast in the dark of the morning, and then I put the tab on my tongue and waited. To pass the time of the hour long come-up, we played a winning game of League of Legends, but halfway in, the effects started.

The first thing happened while I was sitting at my desk. My hands had a profound feeling of floating on the keyboard in conjunction with the sensation of relaxing heaviness throughout my entire body. I felt incredibly euphoric after finishing the video game, but questioned whether I would feel the same had we lost. Regardless, excitement bubbled within me, and I said to Dakota that we should go hang out in the backyard now to watch the sunrise.

Upon opening the slider and stepping out onto the back deck, nothing seemed particularly odd. The morning was a bit overcast, and though the stained wooden fence and green grass had a bit more vibrance to them, things seemed normal. The two of us sat for a few minutes, and as I expressed my eagerness to Dakota, I noticed he too was craving fun. I watched him pull out a plastic green doob tube and dump out a perfectly rolled joint. He raised one eyebrow and looked at me before sparking up and relaxing back into his chair. The morning was serene.

I remembered that I needed water and caffeine, and so I went back inside for a moment and got my liquids. I carried my cups to the slider, and upon opening the door, stepped into a colorful world. Everything in my backyard had very clear edges. My visual acuity had increased significantly, and I specifically noted the large locust tree in the middle of the yard. Its bark was incredibly detailed and appeared to flow like a slow river. I looked at the sky and noted how beautiful a day it was, and back down at my hands seeing how they appeared to glow. Everything was great, and I wanted to make it better, so I decided to smoke some weed.

    Dakota was happy to smoke more, so he went inside and quickly returned with a two and a half foot bong. He smashed a few hits and then handed the piece my way, bearing a contagious smile. I packed up some Strawberry OG from the dealer down the road and took two big hits while cradling the piece in my lap. The smoke was delicious, like a Hawaiian breeze mixed with sour candy. My brain seemed to float out of my skull and the weed did exactly what I had hoped for. I passed the bong back to Dakota, and felt no worry. The day was beautiful, perfect for enjoying some tasty coffee, crisp and fruity bud, and double dipped LSD.

    I was about two hours into the experience when I had a profound sensation of being intensely high. The heavy body effect had increased, and as I sat in the deck chair, I watched the whole world around me begin to move. The bark of the tree grew and shrank, and the grass flowed like water. I felt very light headed and spacey, and watched a play of powerful thoughts and ideas in my mind. I heard the sound of geese overhead, and began to wonder about people forcing this creature to migrate. I contemplated how hard on nature and the world humans are, and how much privilege I had living in a first world country. I thought about how significant an impact my freedoms had on nature, and how I was directly contributing towards climate change. Guilt and feelings of dread percolated in my heart, wearing on my mood and completely changing the vibe.

I shot up out of my chair and blurted, "I want to do something!"

"What do you want to do?" Dakota asked.

"I want to move somewhere! I want to go!"

I went inside, found my mom, and told her that I wanted to go to the woods. She said she needed some time to get ready, but agreed to bring us. I felt a great sense of urgency to get to nature; I really wanted to move and do something. Minutes later, the three of us were in the car and on our way to a forested park at the end of town.

I had a great impatience riding in the car. It seemed to be taking an absolute eternity to get out of the city, and as I watched as car after car go by, I could not believe how many people there were. Traffic was followed by orange construction cones, and I watched uncomfortably while the blight of the city dragged. Then, I looked at the clock which read 9:02 AM, and began to experience a moment of infinity. Time stood completely still, but I feared not. This was certainly a characteristic of time, and I chalked it up to LSD simply pausing everything for a moment.

Once we had finally made it to the woods, I was overjoyed to get out of the car. I had an overabundance of energy, and was eager to see what kind of a beautiful trip nature held. Unfortunately, it had rained the night before, and there were tons of mosquitos. They buzzed all around us the second we hit the trail, and each time I would feel the sensation of tiny legs or a bite, I would hit and wipe that part of my body. I became stuck in the thought loop of getting bit and trying to wipe away the mosquitos. I was in agony, focused only on getting to the end of the trail, and wishing I had just stayed home instead of coming to this insect-ridden place.

We had not driven all this way to turn back though, so I insisted on making it through the forest and the three of us quickly pushed down the trail. Then the love of my life texted me and I felt overwhelmed with emotion. Joy came first, followed by primal worry stemming from recent episodes of doubt. Whether it was the fact that we were long distance, or I lacked trust, or I was simply overcome by the powerful effect of love, I could not contain my feelings. I began texting her and crying because of my doubt, and remembered how often I had second guessed myself. She was everything in the world to me; how could I ever think she was not the one? In the midst of this anxious experience, my mother interrupted me and said: "Well, hey, isn't it a beautiful day?"

"Yeah, I guess it is."

I looked up at the sky and saw the contrast of green spiky pine tree tops against the pure-blue sky. This image morphed into a geometric pattern, and I could not believe how beautiful a day it truly was.

"Why are you crying?" she asked.

"I'm just dealing with something right now."

Dakota was on the path ahead, suffering from mosquitos and eager to get back home. I was conscious of the fact that we needed to move, but I was so preoccupied with my feelings for my girlfriend that I could only focus on that. I ran through the woods while staring down at my phone, and eventually made it back to the car, having missed out on the glory of the woods experience entirely.

I texted my girlfriend during the entire car ride home, and once we had made it there, Dakota and my mother went inside, and I went out into the garage. I sat in a plastic chair looking out a dry wooden window crawling with big spiders. I called up my girlfriend and talked to her for three to four hours, and finally resolved my prior doubts. I concluded that I was incredibly happy in this relationship and that I wanted dearly to make it work. I realized that I had been telling her and myself things that brought unnecessary drama. These were untruths that hurt both myself and her, bringing worry and fear not because they were rational, but because they spiked adrenaline. This call felt like it connected me so deeply with her, and dispelled what had been months of tormenting anxiety.

The call ended around 2 pm, and I felt a deep sense

of peace and love. My worry was gone, so now I could enjoy and ride out the rest of this LSD trip. I did feel like I had abandoned Dakota, but thought he would understand. I went back inside to find him lying face down on the couch, nearly passed out.

"What's wrong?" I asked.

"I'm really tired."

My mom saw me in the living room, and noticing I had been crying, asked what was wrong.

"It was this thing with the relationship, but we figured it out. I feel a lot better now."

"You should take a shower. It will make you feel better."

I thought that this was a great idea, and made my way to the bathroom. I avoided looking at myself in the mirror, and had to come to terms with the fact that I was getting naked. I figured no one would come barging in, so I stripped down and hopped into the shower. I focused on the sensation of warm water running down my back, and looked at the detailed tile lining the shower. It was a river-rock brown with streaks of beige and black running through flinty textures. I was lulled as geometric patterns formed and breathed in the rock. The call with my girlfriend had been cathartic, and my mind danced with how happy she made me. Then, I noticed a figure begin to form in the granite and watched as it evolved and became more detailed until it was very clear that this was in fact my girlfriend. She swooned about in the rock, flowing naturally and turning her head.

"No way, no way!" I said as the rock manifestation of the one I loved moved as if alive. My eyes feasted on the effect until the wall returned to normal and I was left staring at the same tile I had always seen. The shower was a perfect choice, and now I finally felt like I had a level of stability. Then I remembered that one of the things I really wanted to do was lay in my bed and listen to music while watching closed-eye visuals. I dried off and put on some clothes and headphones before laying down in bed to listen to some Shpongle. My peak had already come and gone, and I was not as high as I wanted to be to listen to trippy music. The visual effects were absent, and the music sounded like it always did. Unimpressed, I took off my headphones, and returned to the living room to see Dakota packed up, ready to leave. His impending departure gave me a sense of sadness. I wanted to enjoy the trip with my friend and share the fun that was happening, but things did not go as planned. We said our goodbyes, and then it was just my mother and I.

There was a festival by Wilx park that day, and though I wished I were tripping harder for this event, it still sounded like a lot of fun. I enjoyed the car ride there with my mother, and we wandered around looking at artwork, trinkets and jewelry, and listening to live music. When it began raining after an hour, we took cover in a bakery and enjoyed some homemade frosted doughnuts.

An hour passed and I grew tired of being out and about and decided I wanted to head back home. This was on the come down, and once back home, I went into the basement and took a small hit of weed. This brought on some mild visuals however, it was nothing compared to what I had experienced that morning.

I was disappointed; the experience was not what I had expected. I wanted more visual effects and time to be immersed in the divine feeling of the trip, but, that being said, the best possible thing happened. I was brought a peace that I did not know was possible through confident love. This effect was far more valuable than the others.

The problem with this trip and the ones preceding it was that I always felt like I wanted to take more to experience stronger effects. I had a pipe dream of the perfect psychedelic experience that was just over the horizon. I thought I could reach that state by taking a higher dose, adopting a particular mindset, or following a concrete plan. I never quite got what I was looking for; my experiences would either be underwhelming and a tease of what could be, or far too frightening and plagued with recursive thoughts and dread that distracted from the divine side.

The high levels of the psychedelic realm continue to tempt me to this day, but I know now fear and terror lie in those realms. It takes a truly intrepid psychonaut to commit to those high doses, and a strong mind to make it through. For years I chased what I thought was a feeling brought on by the psychedelic experience, only to realize that these substances were stimulating my past memories. Distinct moments in childhood, hazy pictures of the past, and great feelings of wonder came not only from LSD, but cannabis as well. I thought for a long time that something important was hidden in these images and feelings, but I came to realize that there was a parallel between childhood and the psychedelic experience. Of course, substances that replicate lifes early developmental stages also stimulate memories of those times and so cleverly intertwine the two that they are nearly inseparable.

Chapter 8

Halloween 2017

Stark differences become more apparent between the playful illusions of childhood and the harsh realities of adulthood as we age. Some experiences sober us up to this reality more than others. Sometimes, all that is required is purposeful contemplation, while in other circumstances, an unconsidered perspective may be presented by a mind altering substance. Though both of these channels for realization can bring about great changes in an individual, arguably the most intense changes come about by full immersion in dangerously real experience. Threats to life come in varying levels of complexity and intensity, and in turn require appropriate planning and action. "The unseen blade is the deadliest" from *Zed, League of Legends*. However, attempting to calculate the potential for each moment to present a threat is futile, and results in unparalleled levels of anxiety and psychosis. Ignorance is bliss, but forethought and planning reduce the chances of an event catching you off guard. The line between being ready and being over prepared is a thin one.

    Children and young adults frolic in their sense of unknowing, and are immersed in the present moment. Perhaps that is why these times are revered by those who reflect upon them, and protected by those who understand vulnerability. Regardless of how much one may attempt to cling to a comfortable perception, or how much an authority tries to shelter the truth, it is well known that, eventually, we must wake up. Choosing not to accept the truth only leads to a hindered perspective, and is a dangerous game to play with those who prey upon the weak and ill informed. As sobering of an effect evil has upon the mind, so, too, does truth liberate us from our infantile state and call us to faith that good shall prevail. Refusing to accept the truth of what the world is and cowering behind comfortable perspectives almost always leads to some kind of jarring experience of reality that challenges faith.

•••

The story began in the bedroom of my old house where I was rolling up a joint and enjoying some reggae and contemplating what the night would hold for me. This was my first Halloween since graduation, and it was the only time I was invited to a traditional party with booze, pizza, and awkward teenagers whom I did not know. It was the most cliché venue I could think of: a suburban house with the parents out of town. I wanted to see what it would be like to finally attend a stereotypical teenage drinking party, and I figured three joints and a few grams of ground up weed would suffice for the evening. With that, I gathered my belongings, informed my dearest love of the plan for the night, and then texted my buddy Louis to let him know I was on the way to pick him up.

Upon exiting the comfort of my house into the cold night, I noted the darkness. There was heavy cloud cover and a sharp breeze that rustled the crisp leaves of the sycamore trees. I had no fear of evil that night. A holiday spent with my high school friend Louis, a drive across town to visit with Max before the party, and some good weed: a perfect Halloween night.

I walked to the end of my driveway and opened the door of my 2013 cherry red Dodge Charger. She had only been mine for a little over two months since my birthday, and still had that overwhelming new car effect. The interior was completely black with a soft leather steering wheel and a push-start button that brought to life the fierce hemi engine. I put on some rap with heavy bass, and slowly backed out of my driveway onto the asphalt road lined with towering sycamores. With a little bit of gas, I confidently pulled down the road and made my way across town to Louis's college dorm.

I had to be careful of all of the trick-or-treaters, so I kept my speed reasonable until I made it to the college parking lot. With an opportunity to give her some gas, I gunned it along the curved road, roaring the motor through campus. A brief second of thrill and fossil fuel waste, and then I hit the brakes just outside of Louis's dorm. One impatient minute of waiting and then I saw him walking out of the building, so I turned the music way up so he and all of the other conservative school students knew that I was there.

Louis's form was revealed by street lights. He was a heavyset fellow, around 200 pounds and 6 feet tall. He had medium length dark brown hair, and a short but full bit of facial hair. He was carrying a backpack, a smile, and a box mod vape, exhaling clouds as he made his way over to my car. I turned the music down as he opened the door.

"How's it going?" he asked, tossing his backpack into the rear.

"Hey, it's going well, Happy Halloween" I returned.

"Yeah, Happy Halloween, this party should be a good time," he stated. "We're going to head east first though to catch with Max, right?"

"Yup, he wants us to meet him by the bar on the corner. He didn't give an exact address." I answered.

"I wonder if he's living in a new apartment or renting something over there," Louis offered. "Guess we'll find out."

And with that, we were off into the night. The party was not starting for at least another two hours, so we would have some time to see what Max had been up to since graduation. There had been a recent story in the news involving him and a former classmate's involvement in an assault of an older gentleman, but we wanted to get the story directly from him. There had even been a clip of him testifying in court, and it seemed entirely unreal that one of our friends had gotten caught up in some kind of legal case.

I sped at every opportunity available as Louis and I blew vape clouds out the windows, leaving dissipating white trails of glycol residue. Loud rap music and adrenaline dominated the atmosphere as the seats gripped our bodies through sharp turns. We eventually came upon the brick roads of East that were lined with century old houses and dilapidated outbuildings. Mauve and teal paint contrasted with weathered whites and brick porches while hippies lingered around houses and local bars. Outside the place we had been told to meet Max, there was a line of a dozen Harleys, each marked with unique features like steel skulls and large tailpipes.

"Well, there it is. I don't see him," I stated, slowly cruising past.

"Let's park and get out, then he'll probably see us," Louis suggested.

I scanned the lot near the Harleys for parking, and spotted a space further down the brick road. Then a squawking shout came from a house we were passing, and I figured I was being heckled for my car. I looked out the window to see Max sitting on the porch with a tight hood pulled over his head. I understood the command and parked just outside the house. Louis and I jumped out of the car and made our way over to Max.

He met us on the porch holding a bottle of fireball whiskey in one hand, puffing a joint in the other.

"Wassup," he garbled, leaving the joint in his mouth. This and a hand slide and fist bump were the extent of the greeting formalities before Max passed the joint to Louis. There we were, sharing a smoke session on a random porch somewhere in East. Then the door to the house burst open and my eyes darted to a stocky, short-haired blond guy lingering in the doorway. He had an intoxicated look pasted on a dull, block shaped face.

"Yo, Max, lemme get a hit," he said.

"Nah, you been fiending tonight. Go roll up some of your own shit," he retorted with a venom that I was not sure was authentic or sarcastic. Max had a very quick temper but would also mellow out in a matter of seconds. I never really knew if he was genuinely upset, but testing him was a mistake.

"Quick being a BITCH, bro, and let me take a hit. That's probably my stuff you rolled up anyway," he spat back.

"Fine, fiendin ass," Max said as he handed the joint over.

"Oh, this is Charlie. He's living here with me and a couple other guys who are gone."

"Sup," Charlie choked out as he exhaled a puff of the joint.

Louis and I murmured an introduction, and after this guy had taken multiple puffs, he passed me a roach with one resiny hit in it. I figured it impolite to deny, so I took one lousy hit and passed it back to Max who cashed it on the porch. Then he took a swig out of the fireball and made a peculiar statement.

"Gotta stay incognito. There's gangs out here."

My face scrunched in disbelief, and I looked at Louis who shared my confusion.

"Wait, why?" Louis asked.

"They are hunting me cuz' I testified against Henry in court."

I scoffed at the lie; Max had to be joking. I stared at him with a look of disbelief to let him know I was not buying it, but his face was serious. He was genuinely scared and trying to remain anonymous because he was a witness to an assault and murder. Now Henry's gang members had a score to settle with Max. I figured there was more of the story to tell, but Max was silent. Then Charlie chimed in. "That's why we're at this house; they don't know we're here."

I looked at Max for another quiet moment and waited for him to crack. Nothing; he was afraid and dousing his anxiety in booze.

Charlie read Louis and my disbelief well and continued about how he had seen people following them over the past week. What motive did either of them have to lie? I started to believe the story; Louis and I were in the company of two gang targets.
Before I could act on my desire to flee to the car, Max and

Charlie were inviting us in to take a look at the house. I was high and paranoid, but curious; these two fellows had more stories to share. I did not know if I would get the chance to see either of them again, be it at a funeral or in prison, so against my instinct to abandon the company of these delinquents, Louis and I followed them into the house.

A short hallway painted bleak white opened into a large living room. Two big beanbags lay plopped on the pasty carpet next to a grayish leather couch aimed at a large TV. Louis and I were guided to the couch where I remained tense and very aware of all of the metal blinds on the windows around me. Max slouched into one of the beanbags and Charlie lingered near the edge of the room, peeking out the window through slits.

"Are you sure they don't know you're here?" I asked solemnly.

"Yeah, I'm not trying to get shot!" Louis chimed in.

"Don't worry, if they firing in, we firing out." Max assured us.

He must have a gun somewhere in here; I do not think he's kidding. I suppose that is better than being unarmed sitting ducks. Tonight was truly living up to Halloween's flavor of fear, but this fact soothed me because it kept the possibility of fiction open. The situation was almost too cliché; something had to be staged.

The silence was broken with superior rap music and

rhythm that pleased my high mind. Bass drops gave me goosebumps while I thought about smoking more. I was euphoric but plotting an escape plan in case of calamity. Then I saw Max appear in the doorway of the living room wielding a shotgun. He had a sinister grin on his face and aimed the gun with one hand towards Louis and me; the rap music poetically thumped the speaker. I felt a deep vulnerability and embarrassment, but I was not worried about his intentions. I believed he was holding the firearm simply to show us that his story was no joke and that he was prepared to fight.

 Thankfully this moment was brief. Max had gotten his message across, and I followed his gaze over to Charlie standing next to the window who also had a smug grin on his face. The rap music continued to blare until it became apparent that Louis and I had questions about the case with Henry, and what had happened that night. Charlie and Max lazed down into the beanbags across from each other, appearing well aware of their dangerous situation. They were unfazed because of excessive substance consumption; their primal was worry muted by intoxication.

 "So, what were you guys doing that night?" Louis asked.

 "Well, Henry and I were out for a night ride when suddenly this guy stopped and started heckling us. We were both Xanned out, and Henry wasn't going to take any shit from this guy. He started punching him and kicking him until he was down on the ground."

"Why didn't you guys just leave?" I asked.

"Henry's got anger management issues and because this guy wouldn't stop talking or trying to get up, he just kept wailing on him."

"There's a point when you've gone too far," Louis stated.

"He didn't have an off switch. I was screaming at him to stop, but he kept kicking him until his chest was caved in, and his face was beaten until you couldn't even see his nose anymore. I even saw his eyeball come out of its socket."

"Damn," Louis said quietly. "Damn."

How horrifying, and still strictly on par with the season of fear. Max's description brought back a memory of a night I spent in my basement with one of Henry's friends directly following the incident. He had pulled up a picture of the victim in a hospital bed and displayed it as if it were some sort of trophy of how brutally this person had been beaten. Utter disgust and anger boiled within me at the lack of self control and cruelty of this troubled person whom I had sat next to in class.

I did not have anything to add; the story was worse than I thought. The rumors about it were dispelled in this moment because I now knew exactly what happened from the person who had witnessed it.

"His entire case fell apart when that guy died from his injuries. Now he's facing a life sentence," Max finished.

"Good! He deserves to rot in prison for that," Louis asserted.

Max abruptly shut off the music, and then he was next to Louis and me on the couch, shoving his phone underneath a pillow. Fear crept up my spine as I wondered if now was the time that the firefight would begin. Charlie remained silent while Max looked intensely at Louis and me.

"Do you know how many people Henry has killed?"

I stared at him.

"He has a 20 person body count, and the guns he used are hidden all around the city. He's part of a hitman gang; those are the people looking for us."

Now this had to be bullshit; there was no way someone could get away with that many murders without being caught. I could not deny, however, the memory of seeing shootings in the news. Then I remembered a very specific afternoon with Kode. He was friends with Henry but told me he was cutting ties after Henry started talking about hiding the guns used in the killings. Even if all of this was true, believing it certainly would not benefit my psyche.

The music turned back on as Max moved his phone out from under the pillow. I realized now that he had done this to prevent microphone tapping, and this made an ever growing ominous vibe linger in the room. If even a little bit of what Max had shared was true, there was no question that he had gotten wrapped up in some evil things with some evil people. I could only imagine his mental turmoil and suffering as a result of this. Who had once been an innocent kid that I had played with in the mud and in whose house I had spent many nights now was involved in gang violence and drug abuse.

The uncomfortable vibe continued to grow in that white living room until Max proposed smoking. Everyone was in agreement, and Louis and I followed them down the hallway to a bleached wooden stairway to the second floor. The old boards creaked under our weight as we climbed, and then there was another narrow hallway lined with bedroom doors. We were led to the end where a weathered wooden door opened to a set of unfinished steps up to a colorfully lit attic. These ones groaned differently as the four of us made it to the top floor of the 19th century house. The ceiling was tall and unfinished with LED Christmas lights strung through the roof boards, and stoner decor covered the walls.

We sat in four camp chairs that were arranged in a square fashion pointed at each other in the center of the room. There was no heat or insulation, and the night breeze bit through the aged wood and ventilated the environment. I sat in my chair and looked more closely at the room: Psychedelic tapestries, a burlap bag that read "premium cannabis," and square frames of kaleidoscopic art were illuminated by the rainbow hue of light strands. Despite the disturbing facts I had learned that night, I felt a peculiar sense of wonder and euphoria with undertones of acid haze.

Max appeared lost in thought as he looked at the different decorations in the room, but he seemed unable to remember exactly how these things had come to be. Objects seemed to stimulate memories, and in the midst of his drug consumption and difficult dilemma, positive emotions connected to lost times were brought about by these items. Wonder crept over me as I watched Max reach behind his chair and pull out a small teal glass bong. I knew there was more to him than what he showed on the surface, and I wanted to have a formal one on one talk so I could understand how he had gotten to this point. Whose house this was, how he managed to get a shotgun, and when in the hell he lost his innocence.

Max packed up the bong, and, after taking a hit, blew smoke up into the air and watched it slowly dissipate in the room. He looked down at me with a grin on his face and said, "Ready to take a rip?"

I nodded and reached over to take the piece that had a completely ashed bowl. I reached into my pocket and pulled out a little plastic container, popped the lid, and pinched off a clump of sticky bud. I packed up the bong, took a hit and held it for a moment before slowly exhaling. The smoke curled and twisted around as it was pushed by a gust penetrating the attic walls. I felt lightheaded with a mild pit in my stomach. I was as far away from an exit as possible, and with only one stairwell down, if one of those hitmen gang members were to find us, it would be a massacre.

I passed the bong and container of weed left to Louis who packed himself a bowl and took a big hit; he passed the bong to Charlie who inhaled a cloud and continued the rotation between the four of us.

"Aside from the whole court case, how have you been since high school, Max?" Louis asked. "It's been months since we've seen you."

Max paused for a minute and then looked at Charlie, and back at Louis.

"It's honestly been crazy, dude. Not even joking, I had $17,000 at the start of summer and I have none of it left."

"How?" Louis interrogated.

"I spent it all on drugs, guns, and clothes."

Silence filled the room for a moment before Max resumed his narrative.

"Yeah, I was trappin hard. I was the supplier of cocaine for our entire school."

"I always knew Kode was selling coke at our school, but you did too?" Louis asked.

"Kode helped me get some of it, but he mostly just sold weed and acid."

I sat in disbelief. My entire senior year I was eating lunch with Max, completely blind to the fact that he was a major drug dealer. Not only that, but our school had a coke ring.

"Are you serious?" I asked.

"There were so many cokeheads at our school. Remember when those underclassmen would come over to our corner and try to talk to me but I would just tell them to fuck off? That was because they were trying to buy and being sketchy about it. All those rich white kids knew I could get it for them."

I bubbled my lips and contemplated this for a few minutes while Max talked about the time he took nine tabs of acid. I compared his description of it to wandering lost through a carnival for twelve hours, but I was unsatisfied with his lack of deeper insight on the experience. Thoughts spun in my head about his criminal and reckless behavior before being interrupted.

"That's not as crazy as what happened to Charlie on Xans though. This nigga died bro."

Everyone looked at Charlie.

"I told you I don't want to talk about that shit bro."

"This dude took too many Xans and was literally dead," Max said as he leaned forward in his chair towards Louis and me.

"Really? What happened?" Louis pressed.

Charlie stared down at the floor with a blank look, and then back at Max.

"I took six schoolbuses and passed out in the back of my parents' car while they were driving. They had to get paramedics and shit."

Max looked back at Louis and me with high eyebrows of realization and compassion. A long few seconds passed and then Charlie began again.

"It was really fucked up."

"What did your parents say then?" I asked.

"They put me into rehab."

"That's good. So you got clean then?" I said.

"Well, I was in this place with a bunch of other hardcore addicts who smuggled in more xans."

"I guess that makes sense." Louis added.

"Yeah, so basically I just got barred out in rehab for a couple weeks." Charlie said with a sheepish grin.

Laughter filled the room. This guy spent weeks in rehab binging on the very drug he was detoxing from. I suppose that is why those kinds of places are a double-edged sword.

"See, I told you this dude's crazy," Max said seriously.

We passed around a few more bowls, and then I began to get a sense that it was time to leave. There was still a party to get to and Max's attention was buried in his phone.

"Do you think I could get a ride? I'm supposed to meet Ron at his place just down the road," Max asked.

"Sure, that's fine. We should probably get going to that party anyway."

Louis agreed, and then Max got up to lead the way. We walked single file down the attic stairwell, back through the narrow white hallway lined with doors, and down the creaky bleached stairs to the front of the house. Max, Louis and I walked out onto the bare concrete porch and looked back at Charlie standing in the doorway.

"I'm just gonna hang here, Max. I'll catch up with you later."

Max nodded and turned back toward the road.

"It was nice meeting you, Charlie, Happy Halloween," Louis adieud.

"Yeah, Happy Halloween, man," I added.

"Nice meeting you guys too. Take it easy."

With that, Charlie shut the door, and the three of us headed over to my cherry-red car waiting patiently in the darkness. I unlocked it, hopped in, and after all the doors were shut, I felt the tightness in my chest loosen. Still, I was in the company of a supposed gang target, but at least I was mobile now. I wondered if a scout had seen Max enter this vehicle and how much I would have to duck to dodge gunfire.

"Where are we going then?" I asked.

"696 Balsam Drive. It's down a couple streets. I'll guide you there."

I brought the engine to life and shifted into drive, sending us off down the dimly lit brick road. My brow furrowed, noticing that there were no trick or treaters, or houses with porch lights on. No decorations or street lights either, just dark sidewalks and driveways that disappeared into shadowy garages. After a turn off the main street, and directions from Max that seemed inefficient, he blurted: "Pull off right up here."

I parked next to a navy blue house propped up on a cement foundation. A thin sidewalk ran up and down the road, and as I was trying to see the address of this house, a large figure spooked me at the passenger side window. He had glasses, medium length black hair, a round and pale white face with pink cheeks, and a stocky torso wrapped in black. By the time I recognized him as Ron, Max had rolled down the window.

"You guys headed to that party tonight?" he asked.

"Yeah, are you?" I asked, silently hoping the answer was no.

"Nah, we're going to a party here."

Max opened the door and stepped out into the night. Then he stuck his head back through the window and said, "See y'all later."

I watched the two of them disappear into the night, heading the opposite direction of the house we had parked at. I cruised to the end of the road and noticed the street name was not the one Max had given us. Why had he brought us to a different address? It must have had something to do with Ron; I had given him a false address to my house a few months back because he was a known felon and crack dealer, and apparently now I had been paid back the favor. I wondered what the rest of Max's night was going to look like, and hoped he would not be a victim of violence. Maybe he was safer with Ron and whatever gang he ran with anyway.

With the dangerous company gone, and some residual fear, it was time to swing by the west side and pick up our buddy TJ before the party. Louis helped me navigate the bumpy winding streets of the east until we made it to the highway, and had some cruise time.

"I can't believe that about Henry. Do you think he actually killed all those people?" I asked, leaning back in my seat.

"Man, I'm not sure. I knew Kode and them were involved in shady shit, but murdering people? That's insane."

"I remember Kode telling me some really suspicious stuff about Henry back in school, but I figured it was just a joke, until now. I'll be honest, I was paranoid as hell in that house," I confessed.

"Me too, man, I wasn't trying to get shot! Max could have been lying or just screwing with us, but he seemed really serious about it. Plus, Charlie was wound up too, and I wouldn't doubt gangs move around that area."

"It does seem kind of convenient on Halloween, but I'm just glad we're out of there now."

I turned up some music, and the two of us toked on our vapes. The nicotine settled my mind, and brought about a feeling of euphoria and a heavy sensation in my body. It also seemed to sober me up from weed, and keep me focused on the road. We cruised across the highway through downtown until the exit came up that led us down a ramp into a densely populated neighborhood. The houses were close together, but tastefully decorated, and illuminated by warm porch lights. Hues of orange and yellow glowed on the black road ahead, and guided the way through town.

A few minutes later, we pulled up outside TJ's house, and I watched as he walked down the long driveway toward the car. He had a tawny messy hair cut, a narrow face; light brown eyes, slightly tanned skin, and a slender figure, shaped like a board. I stuck my arm up and pointed my thumb to the back, and he opened the door and hopped in.

"Sick car dude, I bet this is fast!"

"It's very fast." I said proudly.

"What's up, TJ?" Louis greeted.

"Hey Louis, you ready for this party?"

"Heck yeah, it's gonna be lit."

I eased the car onto the road and took directions from Louis.

"So Jae is hosting the party? Do you know anybody else who's going?" TJ asked

"I think it's just going to be us and a bunch of random people. There's supposed to be free pizza though." I answered.

"Any booze?.

"Yup, that's what he said, but I'm just smoking."

We navigated back to the highway, and now were headed south towards the suburbs. Entirely unfamiliar with where I was going, I depended on Louis to get us there, and soon we were exiting onto a long and dark road. The only light was a gas station a mile down the opposite direction we were heading, bordered by an open field and more unlit asphalt disappearing into the distance.

"Where the heck are we?" I asked.

"This is Huckville; we gotta turn left here." Louis replied.

I craned my neck looking for oncoming traffic, and pulled out onto the 55 mph road. My headlights illuminated a short distance in front of me, revealing endless street bordered by open fields.

There were no other cars here, and I felt very reliant on our navigation system. We came upon a white plastic fence that stretched up around our next turn. Again, the road was long and straight, bordered by no shoulder. Then I saw a stop sign in front of the road to blackness.

"You guys wanna go fast?"

"Hell yeah!" Louis said.

"Hang on!"

I brought us to a stop at the sign, and shifted into manual mode; flipped on the brights, grabbed the wheel at noon, and mashed the gas pedal, screeching the tires and sending us flying. The engine roared and bellowed as I maxed out the RPMs, and satisfyingly droned with a shift into second. Our speed continued to grow: 40, 50, 60; I shifted into third with more gas, causing the engine to rumble into third. Seventy, 80, into fourth gear we went, polluting the quiet fields around us with blasts of fuel. Ninety, how much further would I go? I had to hit a hundred. I did not relent on the pedal until we topped out at 103, and with a burning feeling in my chest and throbbing heart, I pushed the brake and cut the speed in half.

"Holy shit." TJ said.

"That's how fast it gets to a hundred. Awesome," Louis said, ripping his vape.

"These roads are perfect for it. Straight and flat.

Let's just hope there's no cops. Where do we go now?"

"It's just straight for another few miles."

"It seems like we're in the middle of nowhere." TJ said.

"This is the way to the address Jae sent. Not too much further."

I noticed another stop sign up ahead, and felt like doing it again. I brought the car a stop, and said, "Get ready!"

I launched us off into the night again, deriving great satisfaction and fun from the power I held. This car handled amazingly, even at high speeds, and I loved the pull of all-wheel drive. Like being strapped to a rocketship, our bodies were forced into the grippy seats while this metal monster tore down the road. Adrenaline surged through my veins, but a tinge of fear seeded in my stomach. A burning feeling welled in my heart as I reached 80, and I reduced my speed. So much fun, but such possible dire consequences. I did not want to keep spinning the wheel of chance and getting caught or making a mistake, so I decided to keep things reasonable.

"This car is sweet, dude," Tj said

"The all-wheel drive really grips the road, and the hemi motor sounds so good."

"Just don't run out of gas out here," Louis warned.

I nodded, and turned up the music before hearing Louis shout "Turn right here!"

I hit the brake, sending us forward into our seatbelts, and the car careening around the corner onto another unlit road. At the very end, I could see a grouping of lit-up houses on a cul de sac. I slowed down as we got close, and after finding the address, pulled up into the driveway.

"We're in the rich neighborhood, huh?" Tj asked.

"Perfect for a Halloween party. Ready to go in, or do you guys want to vape it out first?" Louis asked.

"Definitely vape it out." I grabbed my nicotine steamer from the cupholder and started with a big inhale.

"Want to try mine, Christian? It's thirty nic." TJ asked.

"Seriously?" Louis said. "That's as strong as you can get."

"I know, it doesn't even get me buzzed anymore."

"Thirty will make me sick, but try this, it's Hawaiian Pog in three," I said, passing back the vape.

"Oh yeah, that's really tasty. No throat hit though." TJ passed it back to me, and then Louis shared too. The three of us sessioned for a few minutes before opening the doors and letting out a plume of thick cloud that disappeared into the cold night air. With an intense body buzz, slight nausea, and floaty feeling in my head, I followed my two friends up to the porch and stood back as they knocked on the door. A repetitive thumping base was silenced, and a shout came from inside. "Someone's here!"

A few seconds later, the door opened and Jae was standing there with his girlfriend, Ahna. He was shorter than all of us, and had light brown, almond-shaped eyes, bushy dark-brown hair, and a thick five o' clock shadow on a square jaw. Next to him, Ahna was very skinny with tawny skin and jet-black hair. She had a thin face, big eyes, red lips and high cheekbones.

"Hey TJ, I did not know you were coming. What's up buddy?" Jae greeted.

"Christian invited me. They came and picked me up."

"Hell yeah, come on in, guys."

We followed the two of them past an open room on the front of the house into a kitchen with a large granite island filled with a rainbow of alcohol. Hard lemonade, cinnamon whiskey, beer, and flavored vodka were arranged among piles of individually wrapped candy. Separated by a bar, the kitchen led to a big entertaining area with a giant flatscreen TV, and half a dozen unfamiliar teenagers. Jae turned the music back up which was rap with heavy bass, and then grabbed a slice of pizza out of a greasy box sitting on the counter.

"Want some pizza or beer?" he shouted over the music.

TJ and Louis picked beers off the table, and I grabbed some pizza. It was barely warm, and cheap, but delicious. I thoroughly enjoyed it and stood around chatting with my friends. We had not been introduced to the other people at the party and they appeared to be occupied with some sort of game, so we lingered in the kitchen, grazing on the free food. I noticed Jae had disappeared, only to see him return a few minutes later from an unknown part of the house.

"We're gonna go out and smoke. You guys want to come?"

I looked at my two friends nodding and shouted "sure." We followed Jae back past the room on the front of the house, but now there were two guys in their twenties sitting on a couch, watching us walk by. They were dressed conservatively, and I wondered if they were watching over the house.

"Who are they?" I asked Jae as he closed the door to the front porch.

"The girl who goes to Hucksville High School who's throwing this party, they are her brothers. They're chill though."

In addition to Louis, TJ, Jae, Ahna and I, the porch the porch had three other people on it: a lanky guy with long brown hair and a backwards hat, a short girl with bobbed blonde hair and a round face, and this guy named Jaren whom I remembered from a few months ago at Jae's house. He had short, spiky hair, glasses, and a slim build, but my memory of him was sour. When I met him before, all he had talked about was how satisfying it would be to kill this guy he worked with, especially because he was a bodybuilder. What a freak.

"You must have brought some weed, Christian," Jae said.

"Yeah, I got a couple joints." I pulled out a green tube and slid a loosely wrapped joint into my hand. I sparked it up, and then began the rotation. By the time it was back to me, there was nothing but a roach, so I sparked another and passed it around again. I distantly played in the conversation amongst the group until I noticed Jae get up and silently leave the group with Jaren. The others did not seem to take notice, so I asked Ahna, "Where did he go?"

She smiled while looking off in the direction they had walked. I could faintly see them in the distance, until they disappeared into the darkness behind what appeared to be a shed.

"Oh, they do that all the time. It's just bro love."

The group was silent for a moment before resuming conversation as if nothing had happened. Ahna continued smiling in their direction, and I stared at her, wondering if she meant they were engaging in some homoerotic behavior. Odd; she did not seem the type to vibe with a polygamous relationship, but I decided it was probably something she found arousing.

I was sure glad that *I* had a traditional relationship rather than some type of profligate trio. I tried to push the idea of Jae and this guy sucking face out of my head, and tuned back into the conversation. Nothing interesting, just uncomfortable and forced dialogue with strangers. Whether it was my hyperawareness because of cannabis, or the lack of awareness brought on by these people's alcohol consumption, it seemed as though I was the only one concerned with what was going on out in the yard. Then I saw Jae and Jarren reappear on the porch, acting noticeably "normal."

"You guys got more weed?" Jae asked, interrupting the unimportant conversation.

"I do, but I gotta roll it up," I said.

"Can you?" TJ asked.

The attention of the group shifted towards me, and I felt an odd sense of pride. I was the only one with weed, and they were all depending on me to roll a joint. I tried to conceal my ego and said "Can I do it inside? It will be easier to do it on a table."

"Yes, go for it!" Jae said excitedly.

Eager to demonstrate my superior rolling skills, I let myself in through the front door and walked past the two guys sitting in the living room. Their vibe was unreadably uncomfortable. What did they think about weed? I figured it better to ask them than just be some random guy caught rolling on the kitchen counter.

"Is it cool if I roll in here?" I asked loudly.

The TV volume was turned down and one of them shouted, "just don't smoke it in here."

"I was going to smoke outside, but just roll in here," I explained.

"That's fine."

The TV volume went back up, and I hastily began rolling the joint. I knew nothing about these two strangers other than the fact that I was in their house, high. All I wanted to do was get back outside to where I was comfortable, so I rushed through which resulted in a subpar roll. It would still smoke though. I slinked back through the door, trying to not draw any attention from the strangers, and then out onto the porch.

Jae and Jaren had disappeared again, so I leaned up against the vinyl siding and twirled the joint in my fingers. TJ and Louis both had chairs now. I was tired of standing, but I gave a small thanks that I did not have to sit by the girl throwing the party. She gave off sultry vibes blended with intoxication, and I had absolutely no interest in sharing conversation or "getting to know her." TJ was doing that, awkwardly so, and so I kept to myself, daydreaming about my love.

Eventually Jae returned, and Jaren followed shortly after.

"Got the joint?"

I held and sparked it, passing it to Jae who took a big puff, then coughed it out with a laugh. "I can't believe you're smoking weed. I never thought you would in high school. You used to be so against it," he said, passing the joint left.

I took a moment to think about this and said "I never thought I was going to either."

Then the guy with long brown hair wearing the hat thanked me earnestly for the weed; the others followed with less fervor. I felt a sense of generosity and happiness in sharing. If it had not been for marijuana, I never would have shared these moments with these people. This would be our first and last interaction, but for this moment in time, we shared a state of elevation, regardless of relationship, social standing, or our pasts.

One by one, people left the group to go back inside until it was just Louis, TJ, and I. I had finally gotten a seat and was enjoying the night air, but Louis and TJ decided to head back inside for a drink. I was alone for a few minutes before TJ came back out, holding a beer.

"Where's Louis?" I asked.

"He was hanging with the other people playing some Wii. I think they have Super Smash Brothers."

"Oh dude, I love that game. Want to go play?" I asked.

"Yeah, that's why I was coming out here. Let's go."

I followed him back to the kitchen where I indulged on chocolate candy and more pizza while watching everyone sitting in the living room staring at the big-screen TV. I was quite happy – the night was going well, and although it was not the crazy party I had expected, I enjoyed the company on this Halloween. Stoned, savoring pizza and candy, and watching drunken teenagers mingle and struggle with hand-eye-coordination – what more could I ask for. Despite all the insane things Max had described, and the dread of being hunted by a gang, things were shaping up.

Then I heard a scream come from outside the front of the house. It sounded like Jae, and it sounded fake. Then, I heard it again from Jae, and then what sounded like Jaren. Perplexed, I walked out of the kitchen towards the front door and saw Jae come barging in.

"There's a clown! There's a fucking clown!" he said, running past me over to the rest of the party. "There's a clown, it almost got Jaren!"

I raced to the front door, and after putting my shoes on, peered out the front glass and saw Jaren running up to the porch

"Is he serious?" I asked.

With a stone-cold look on his face, he said "It looked exactly like a clown." Someone turned the music down, and the party became silent and tense. Jae ran back into the front room, looking out the window.

"I see it, right there!" he shouted. The whole party ran to the front of the house and looked out into the night. Then another shout came from the kitchen, "There's another one!"

Once again, the party shifted back into the main room while I stayed put, looking out the window. Seconds seemed like hours, but I still was not sure if a clown was even there. I was ready to bolt to my car at a moment's notice, even if it meant evading some kind of lunatic outside.

My mind raced as time went on. There had been at least a dozen stories of clowns in the news this past year, and my thoughts just kept adding evidence to fuel the fire. Here I was, alone, just a few feet from the front door, trying to decide what to do. I heard a slider door open and someone shout "It's a clown! It's a clown!" I lunged toward the door and stole a look back to see if anyone would join the escape. The blonde girl was running straight towards me, and I was halfway onto the porch holding the door open when I saw her make a U-turn and head straight up the stairs.

Dumbfounded, and figuring natural selection was coming for her, I backed out of the house, pushed the front door closed and scanned the front yard. No white faced killers yet, but I was not sticking around to see them. I sprinted to my car, jumped in the front seat, and locked the door.

I started the car and waited to see if either of my friends had escaped. Then the front door came flying open, and Louis appeared with a bright red face and look of immense fear. He came barrelling towards the car, tapping on the hood as he raced to the passenger door. I hit the unlock button, and he jumped inside, immediately locking after.

Scanning little of what was visible in the dark yard, I frantically asked "Was there a clown?"

"There was something there," he said with a face of terror.

"Really?"

"I saw something there, and I booked it. I'm glad we got the plan, though."

"I wasn't going to leave you man. Do you know if TJ is coming? I'm ready to get out of here."

"I'll try calling him."

Louis dialed TJ, and after he picked up said, "Are you going to get out of there, dude? We're waiting in the car."

I heard some unintelligible rambling, and saw a look of confusion appear on Louis's face.

"What's he saying? Tell him we're not going to wait much longer!" I said desperately.

"TJ, get out here, man! We're leaving!"

More rambling followed, and then Louis looked at me and said, "He's trying to fight the clown."
"Are you joking? Let me talk to him!"

Louis put the phone on speaker, and all that could

be heard was the distant voice of TJ shouting about attacking the clown with a beer bottle, and intermittent static. With our friends fate sealed, and the rest dead, or too stupid to join us, I began backing down the driveway. Any clown trying to stop us would be run over, and just as I was near the end of the driveway, I saw Jae come sprinting out of the house towards the car. I stopped and unlocked the door, ready to save one more life tonight, but instead of getting in, he tapped rapidly on the window. I cracked it, and he whispered, "It's a prank, it's a prank! Play along!"

Jae ran back into the house, and I pulled up further into the driveway, still suspicious of the situation. I remained in the car with Louis until a few minutes had passed, and then I saw Jae appear once again in the doorway.

"Guys, it's okay. It's a prank. Come back in."

I shut the motor off and stepped back out into the cold night. I scanned the yard while I made my way to the front door, while Jae snickered "You guys were really scared, weren't you?"

Louis and I remained silent while Jae led us back into the kitchen. Sure enough, there was a guy standing in a carnival suit with a clown mask sitting on the table next to him. He held a blunt weapon, and was surrounded by the other members of the party. Jae could not stop laughing, and TJ stood next to the clown guy, looking at him through slitted eyes while sipping from a beer bottle. I could tell by the expressions on the partygoers faces which ones had been in on the prank, and which ones were the victims. Even the girl who was throwing the party had been pranked, and her previous expression of primal fear had been replaced by one of apparent relief and self consciousness.

The pranksters reveled, while we victims conceded our fear, and though I felt betrayed, the novelty of the experience was amusing. Obviously, Jae did not know where Louis and I had been earlier in the evening, or about our preexisting uneasiness. Or maybe he did, and that made it all the better.

I had been through enough fear this evening, and even though I acknowledged that it was a good prank, I was ready to go home. The purpose of the party to scare the hell out of everybody had been successful, and now it was over. So I said farewell and thanks to Jae and company for the party and returned to my car with Louis and Tj.

The drive back to TJ's house was relatively quiet; we did not talk much. Just the sounds of calming nicotine delivery, a hemi motor purring down the road, and quiet metal cutting through air. I eased into a blissfully detached attitude as the three of us joked about the party, and frolicked in the novelty of the season of fear. By the time we had made it back to TJ's, it was around 2 am, but Tj invited Louis and me in to see his place and unwind.

We did not hang for long, maybe an hour. TJ was five more shots deep, buzzed on nicotine, and crawling around on the floor like a worm. Louis and I watched him while enjoying generously given pastries from the kitchen, reminiscing on times we had been that high. An urgency arose in me as the clock ticked past 3 am, and I felt it was time to get back home into bed and call it a night. Louis and I said our goodbyes to TJ who appeared to be making the floor his bed tonight. We let ourselves out the door, back into the cold night and into the car.

Louis and I earnestly discussed the bizarre night between vape hits, soothing our souls with engulfing rap music. It must have been 3:30 before I was dropping him off at the dorms and saying a short but meaningful goodbye. It went unspoken, but because of all we had been through that night, we had formed a special comradery. We had shared a traumatizing experience, and just as war breeds brotherhood, so too had we become brothers in suffering.

Louis was nothing short of a remarkable ally and my best friend in these times. I spent countless days with him after this night, reliving it and feeling bound together through our experience. As time passed and life unfolded, I pulled away from my friend. I suffered from paranoia and an extreme self awareness that polluted our relationship to the point that I feared him. This fear came from my lack of self discipline. I felt threatened by his knowledge, and ultimately by my inability to accept my own flaws.

There is no question that psychoactive substances contributed heavily toward my mental state of distrust for many people in my life. If I could go back, I would stop myself from the trains of thought I entertained and spare myself the drug experiences that invoked these terrible suspicions.

I can't though, so I, and those affected, are forever changed by what has happened. I will never forget the experiences I have shared with those people who have moved out of my life, nor the lessons they have taught me. Through my suffering, the skills I have learned for coping and being prepared are unmatched. I fervently wish that I could have come out of these times with my relationships intact, but to this day I solemnly grieve the loss of my friendship with Louis.

We shared many more experiences together after this one, and our years of great friendship will be immortalized in these chronicles. As the patterns of existence follow cyclical intensity, Louis and my story will continue in this book, and the sequel.

128

Chapter 9

Hidden

The damage to creativity caused by the ceaseless assertion of realism and denial of subjective experience is unparalleled. The human condition is magic in its entirety, and by embracing the unique powers of the spirit, our ability to transcend and connect with celestial consciousness comes forth. No evidence has been able to disprove the infinity hypothesis or the concept of limitless creation. In realizing this, the mind sees its potential. The spirit, coming from eternity, has the power to bridge the mind with the oceans of heaven. It is capable of harnessing the primordial elements of creation, and forming universes of all kinds. The conception of this power becomes apparent as the mind is made aware of its limitless nature and unbound thoughts. Our spirit has always had this power because it is closer to God. However, if fully revealed, the information would be overwhelming. In this way, our minds drink from the fountain of the divine, slowly. The great potential for jubilation and magnificent love lies within all of us, and by cultivating our connection with the spirit, these things will manifest.

Conversely, realms of darkness and evil can be accessed via the mind's connection with the spirit, yielding the appropriate results. So, too, are those parched of the spirit, who seek to quench their thirst via earthly things. A true connection with the divine comes in different ways to different people; but free will oils the gears of change for everyone. Some may be deluded, while others seek fast glory and carnal pleasure. But do not be mistaken: the war is not against the spirit, rather the mind. The mind is the vector by which celestial consciousness can impact the world, and assuredly, angels of light and demons of fire circle our earthly dimension. They manifest in different ways, brought into the world by people that have materialized a branch of infinity. Because of this, those who seek control battle against attempts to incarnate infinity, both for fear of destruction and desire for power.

The human is the technology capable of greatness, rather than externalities. On earth, as spiritual beings inhabiting physical vessels, our consciousness plays in this dimension for a time before moving on to the next. In this way, we come to realize a degree of purpose: How shall we go about programming our minds to best bring forth the branch of infinity that our spirit desires? This is where the conflict takes place, as others see their intentions as superior. Whether the desire is rooted in personal gain, fear, envy, anger, or simple evil, forcing our will upon others is the ultimate demonstration of ego. Those who are deluded into believing that the self is the ultimate authority will take actions to preserve and nourish it, regardless of the impact on others. The major oversight with exclusively fulfilling the will of the self is that the temporal nature of life means that each person has a unique experience and opportunity for meaning. These opportunities differ greatly, as infinity demands, but denying someone this meaning is insensitive to the fact that another's perspective is impossible to fully comprehend. It also weakens spiritual expression, breeds resentment and consequently results in the same fate: Ego-rooted attempts to control and pursue one's self interests. A truly perfect world is one in which each person can fully express their spiritual infinity without hurting the ability of others to do so.

    Life is not perfect, and many inequalities exist across the multifaceted human experience, so the struggle for universal spiritual actualization continues. Again, however, all humans have the ability to connect with infinity through the mind. Certainly, individuals who seek to inhibit this process are of evil intent, as are those who desire to eliminate such opportunities. All humans deserve respect for the spirit, and should be given the canvas for its expression. The platform for such things is neither monetary nor physical, rather a freedom of thought. The fact is that people must go through different challenges to reach that freedom, but only through such pressure can the diamonds be created. Nothing compares to the product of tenacity, and because it is impossible to fully comprehend or create another's experience, such treasures can only come from that place.

    The tremendous question of why dominates the floor when the spirit is brought up, as does the notion of a creator. Put simply, experience would be boring if we were not a participant. So, through countless existences we roam, feeling and seeing what we are. From stardust we became, and to it we return. As a product of cosmic ingredients, our physical form will inevitably turn back to raw matter, and will never be wasted or lost. So, too, if consciousness is a product of stardust, it will be returned to the dough of creation, but never lost. In that way, we become the elements of genesis, and realize our ability to create infinitely.

Too often, the assertion of consciousness as being finite ignores the fact that the body remains a part of the universe. If consciousness is exclusively a product of the body, how can one stay while the other is lost? It is like suggesting that a burned book means the total loss of its content. The universe does not waste, and energy can be neither created nor destroyed, and so consciousness will go somewhere. The real question is where, made only more challenging by the fact that the spirit is not bound by physical laws nor the confines of death. It is transdimensional, and its destination cannot be tracked. Voyaging to that realm before death is possible through meditation, dreams, psychedelics, and other forms of consciousness exploration. By these methods, we access a part of infinity. We are reminded of the nature of creation, and astounded in seeing the sheer amount of possibile creation. Truly, our spirit unites with the ocean of the consciousness, returning home to where it came from. In returning, the spirit sees the uniquely beautiful aspects of creation. Then, the finite nature of its time here is realized, and the details must be savored. The force of love takes over, and then comes the time to express a unique branch of infinity.

The ethereal is not beyond, but rather all around. We are in the midst of artfully blended spectrums, exploring a three-dimensional reality through the restrictions of our bodies. The immediate perceivable matter surrounding is a result of what our sensory systems can detect, but even that is an illusion. These avenues for sensing are not evolved to detect the full spectrum of reality but rather the fundamental components essential for survival. From ultraviolet light to radio waves and sound frequencies, a staggering portion of our reality cannot be fully perceived. So, despite having instruments to detect these branches of creation, our experience is not all encompassing. Therefore, our conclusions and explanations of reality are imperfect and short-sighted. The perceived benefit and impact of our actions are measured by the limits of our three dimensional reality, and thus the full scope of our actions cannot be fully seen. Spiritual practice is a prime example of this, as a critic may not recognize the immediate benefits of dogmatic practice with their five senses, yet the practioncier imprints on a different level. This rule permeates every part of existence, and thus affirms the notion of the interconnectedness of everything. No action comes without consequence, even if said consequence happens on a different level of the macrocosm.

The spaces we inhabit are affected by the events of the universe, similar to a web warped by the weight of matter. The impact of such happenings can be measured by sensory observation, scientific instruments, and spiritual attunement. Thus, there are points in space where our senses, science, and spirit can all detect some kind of impression from history. This is why certain places feel particularly unique, even without any immediate physical phenomena. Whether in a house of worship or holy land, there is no question that humans can detect hyperdimensional locations. These places exist around the world and have been used for millennia as gateways to interdimensional travel.

The word "travel" is misleading, however, as it implies moving to a different physical area. The reality is that, with infinity all around us, broadening our perspective allows us to see more of what we are already in. This is why exploring consciousness is beneficial to an individual's experience of reality because doing so involves that which they are participating in but do not have an immediate perception of.

Chapter 10

Mom's Dope

Ten years of swimming and a few nasty falls off my longboard caused a nagging pain in my shoulder that came and went with certain activities. This became a major problem in the last two months of my senior year of swimming and brought me a great deal of frustration and hopelessness. Not only was I pressuring myself to perform the absolute best to finish the season, but my coaches and team were also depending on my participation. Physical therapy and careful practice helped only marginally, so I sought relief elsewhere. Weed was the next best option.

I had a fair amount of internal conflict about smoking weed in my early stages of exploration. I knew it was relatively safe, assuming I did not get caught with it, but I was concerned about what my mother thought of my use. Being an only child, I was very close with my mom and did not want to harm our relationship. I did not want to lie to her, as I figured that would only bring further conflict and problems down the road. So, after my first experience with marijuana, I decided I would just ask her if it was okay if I used to help my shoulder. Surprisingly, she said yes, and shortly after, Slater was on his way over with a vaporizer to share in getting loaded.

I waited excitedly in the living room staring out the picture window on the front of the house into the growing evening. My first experience with marijuana had been tremendous fun and I was eager to get better acquainted with it. I had no idea how having my mother's permission would alter the session, but I figured it was just another layer of security and reassurance that what I was doing was okay. I felt quite privileged; most teenagers have to hide and lie about their use, while I could just be honest without fear of punishment. This felt entirely incongruent with the stereotypical teenage rebelliousness, but I figured it was better to be unruffled by worries of parental intervention.

I spotted Slater strutting down the sidewalk towards our house, so I hopped up off the couch and hurried to open the front door. He was just stepping up to the concrete porch when I opened the door and he said, "You ready to get baked?"

"Yeah, man, my shoulder has been bugging me all day."

"All the more reason to get high," Slater said as he stepped into the landing. "And your mom is cool with this?"

"I asked her if I could to help my pain and she said yes."

"Weed is medicine, I use it every day!" Slater snickered as he lazed over to the couch and plopped his backpack on the ground.

I shut the door and then felt a hounding sense of responsibility creep into my mind. Slater's very presence was a liability because of his affinity for drug dealing, not to mention his militant parents who had a strict no tolerance policy. They flushed weed down the toilet, stole his paraphernalia, held back prescribed Ritalin, and one time even hid in the trunk of the car to catch him sneaking out. This just made him use more, despite numerous punishments. I sympathized with his turbulent home life, and though he violated boundaries that put my mom and me at risk, he was my best friend.

Tonight was different than before, though. Now, we were going to be blatantly using a controlled substance in my mother's household. I feared not so much for my safety, but rather hers. She was the responsible adult and the one who would be held accountable if something went wrong. I knew she was entrusting us with a great deal, so I resolved to tread cautiously with my words and actions. Given how fortunate our circumstances were I think Slater understood this too and followed suit.

I sat next to Slater on the couch and watched him pull out a pint jar filled with rich green nuggets of weed flecked with orange. He set it on the couch and continued rifling through his backpack before grabbing a black herb grinder, a large silver battery the size of a hotdog bun, and a glass tube in the shape of a straw. This was everything required to get high, and eagerness wafted over me as I recalled the luscious pine lemon flavors and potent euphoria of my first experience. I wondered for a moment what the interaction would be like if my mom walked out and saw all of this paraphernalia. I knew she had smoked way back in high school and thought she may be impressed by the high tech vaporizer and glass jar packed with fat nugs.

Slater began the session by heating up the silver battery and packing in the glass tube before taking a few long puffs. He smirked and said "It's ready." and handed the piece my way. I could not stop myself from smiling while looking down at the steaming pipe, and took a few deep breaths with pursed lips before slowly inhaling. Musky citrus aromas stimulated my tastebuds, and the sensation of warm vapor filled my lungs. I held it for just a moment until my airway was saturated and then exhaled, letting out an unusually big cloud that led to a tight feeling in my chest and coughing.

"Hell yeah," Slater drawled. I passed the piece back to him while coughing into my elbow before lazing into the couch with my eyes closed. I eagerly awaited the feeling while a warm relaxation wafted over me. The couch felt like it was giving me a big hug and I had no pain in my shoulder. I had no worries or preoccupations-just sheer pleasure in the carnal experience of being high. I felt my eyelids droop and the sense that gravity had been amplified. I stretched my arms up, letting out a pleasant groan, and then noticed that Slater had cached the bowl and was heating up a new one.

"Are we gonna hit another?" I asked hopefully.

"Yeah, you're getting fried tonight." That was exactly what I wanted to hear. My first time in the heavy range had been short lived, and I was ready to explore more of that realm. Slater took a big toke off of the fresh vaporizer and then passed it to me for another round. This time, instead of focusing on the taste, I paid attention to the feeling. The vapor flirted with my lungs as I inhaled aggressively from the tube, causing my clarity to sail away. I had just finished the hit when my mom appeared beside the couch with a smirk on her face, staring down at the paraphernalia scattered on the couch. I quickly handed the vaporizer back to Slater and anxiously anticipated what would come next.

"You little stoners are getting baked out here." she said toyishly. What did this mean? She had said she was okay with it, but was that going to change in an instant? I was in no state of mind to deal with conflict, so I sat silently and waited.

"You want a hit?" Slater asked.

"Sure, load me up. What is that, a vaporizer?"

Was… was she kidding? Was she getting stoned with us tonight? I could not believe my eyes or ears, but sure enough, she sat down next to us on the couch and started toking. I stared at her with wide eyes while she grinned at me in between hits, and in that moment it felt like the entire house was loony. Then, she stood up and walked to the kitchen for a glass of water and came back to say: "You guys want to see something? You're going to shit a brick." She disappeared down the hallway. I looked at Slater, completely bewildered.

"I can't believe we just got high with your mom!" he whispered with lifted eyebrows and a wide grin.

"I know, dude, this is so weird. I'm really stoned too." My mom came back out of the hallway carrying a quart jar, stuffed to the brim with weed. My jaw hit the floor and I watched Slater's eyes grow as he laughed in disbelief.

"What do you think of that?" she said, unscrewing the top. A wave of realization wafted over me as I thought of all the times during my childhood that I had almost caught her smoking. I remembered mornings in her room before school where I could have sworn I smelled smoke, when she had blamed it on her hairspray. Tons of little mysteries I had written off to coincidence and paid no mind to were now revealed. I had so many questions, but the biggest one was how she managed to raise me and go to work every day while smoking weed.

"That's amazing. Can I smell it?" Slater asked. My mom nodded and handed the jar his direction. He took a big inhale and then cocked his head back, letting out a moan. He smelled the jar again and fondled a few of the nugs before giving me a serious look.

"You gotta smell that," he insisted. I took the jar from him which felt like a sin, and then a long smell. It was entirely different from the skunky diesel street weed my friends had been getting. Instead, sweet tangerine citrus aromas blended with a soft organic earthy tone caressed my nostrils. It did not even really smell like weed, more like cutting into an orange on an island beach. I savored another long smell and then handed it carefully back to my mom. Curiosity bubbled about within me, and I wanted to ask her where she had gotten it from. I knew the source had to be kept anonymous though, from Slater at the very least.

"Mind if I pack some up?" Slater asked gingerly.

"Sure, go right ahead." My mom plucked out a green bud from the jar and handed it to Slater who immediately packed it into the vaporizer. After a moment of waiting, I watched her take multiple puffs and compliment the flavor. She continued the rotation to Slater and then to me. This time, the taste was starkly different and smooth, like a finely ground orange peel mixed with a touch of rich soil. The steam came off my tongue sweet, and the novelty of this entire happening occupied all of my attention while my high quickly grew.

I became a bit nauseous and light-headed not long after my third hit while the THC bounced about in my brain. The back of my head felt heavy, and a bit of dull pain irritated my temple and throat before I began to think I was going to throw up. I dismissed myself from the party and hurried to the bathroom where I dry heaved into the toilet a few times before collapsing on the side of it. I felt sick in a way I never had, and it felt like I was fulfilling some kind of cliché. My mom came in to check on me, and I told her I was too high and queasy, but not to worry.

Despite the incredibly unpleasant feeling in my head, everything else was pretty good. Something in the weed made my body feel like I had just finished up a hard workout and now I was resting and recuperating. My bones and muscles felt tranquil, like the impact of swimming every day for years was gone and I was just floating in a great pool of warm goo. Eventually, the urge to throw up left me, and all I wanted to do was go and lay down. I figured that Slater would have no problem with me crashing after tonight's session, so I brushed my teeth and fell into bed. The sheets were inviting, but as I lay on the pillow, the base of my skull radiated a pain down my neck and I felt dizzy. I just wanted sleep, so I focused on the feeling in the rest of my body and drifted off as the sensation of floating overcame gravity.

I woke the next day feeling refreshed and no less curious about weed. The night had been such an odd duality of discomfort and pleasure that I figured it was just some beginner's growing pains. I knew there was still so much more to be discovered, and I was a bit disappointed that I had not been able to enjoy the cognitive effects of the high for longer. I did not know when my next opportunity to smoke would be, but having my mom on board made things much easier. The real question was how far that privilege would go, and what she really thought of weed. We shared a secret now. She was the coolest mom and I wanted badly to brag about her to all my friends, but I had to keep silent. Slater knew he had to as well so that no other parents would find out and we could continue to revel in the great privilege of a safe place to smoke weed.

A great issue surfaced soon after this night. My house was the best place to smoke because there was zero risk of getting in trouble, and the more I experimented with weed, the more people joined in. What started as a small pact between Slater, Bell and me, turned into over a dozen people who knew where the party was. This would have been fine if nobody asked questions but, one by one, they pieced together the puzzle. There was no way to burn through blunts and bongs in the basement without a parent taking notice, so I just told people not to worry. I dealt with guilt and fear as more classmates realized that not only was my mom cool with smoking, but was also a stoner herself. Each new member felt like a betrayal of her trust, but she acted only with compassion and kindness towards me and those joining in.

Such a privilege and environment led to unforgettable experiences with people whom I may never have shared time with otherwise.

Chapter 11

DXMT

On November 18, 2016, I was on the way to buy some dextromethorphan from CVS pharmacy for Louis's birthday. This was the same store I had walked through following the first time I smoked weed and so being in the store it felt delinquent rather than nostalgic. I was here for one purpose: to buy a bunch of capsules of cough suppressant for a drug experience. Not just any "medicine" though. It had to be dextromethorphan without any acetaminophen or guaifenesin. The syrup was also nasty, full of high-fructose corn syrup and dyes. As foolish as it may sound, thirty or so liquigels of the right cough suppressant can bring about a relatively safe night with some dissociation and motor issues. Combinations with diphenhydramine can get pretty wild too, but I was mostly interested in getting some mental schism.

I walked to the back of the store where all the cold medicine was and skimmed over the ingredients, nervous about some suspicious employee accusing me of shopping for a recreational high. I was probably giving them too much credit, though. The average pharmacy worker was unlikely to be well versed with Erowid DXM reports, and besides, if anyone asked, I was getting it for my mom. I found a bottle of twenty of the right capsules, 15 mg each, for just a couple bucks. I grabbed two and, after making my way to the front of the store, casually plopped them on the counter and silently dared the cashier to say something.

Satisfied with a nearly speechless transaction, I grabbed the drugs and headed out the automatic doors into the cracked parking lot. A few feet from my big red charger, I was accosted by a man with dingy clothes.

"Could I get a ride?" he asked, staring at the car.

"No man. I've gotta get home" I opened the door and tossed the DXM into the passenger seat.

"Please, I need a ride. I need to get my kids from daycare and I can't get a hold of my wife."

"No, man, I'm sorry I can't help ya," I said earnestly, trying to get him to bug off.

"Please, I need to get me kids!" he insisted. I lingered outside my door for a few seconds, unable to callously get in and drive away.

"I'll sit in the back if that makes you feel better. Please, it's just down the road." I thought for a few more seconds and remembered the bear spray I had just in the driver's side door. If he were to try anything funny, I could mace him.

"Fine, let's go." I hopped in the driver's seat and looked into the rear until he was sitting right in the middle. He struck me as a bum but with how much faith I had given him, he could pull out a gun and make me go anywhere he wanted. I reluctantly started the car and asked him where to go.

"Pull out onto the main street and turn right. Then it's just a few miles down." I drove quietly and continued glancing into the rearview mirror to see what he was doing. Something about this felt like a lesson, like God had sent a prophet beggar to test my self preservation and cautiousness. Luckily, I had gotten a bum and not a serial killer. Part of me did feel like I was doing the right thing, helping a guy in need pick up his kids. No matter the story though, I knew I had assumed unnecessary and great risk by letting a stranger into my vehicle.

"Turn up here." I pulled off into an apartment complex, wondering where the daycare center was. He guided me a little ways back into it before telling me to park.

"Can I have some money? I gotta pay for the bus to get my kids home."

"No man, I already gave you a ride."

"Please, give me some money. I'll pay you back, I swear." I let out a sigh, figuring the only way to get this guy out of my car was to throw some money at him.

"How are you gonna pay me back?"

"Give me your phone number. I call you and pay you back tomorrow." I highly doubted this, but gave him the benefit of the doubt. Maybe he would, maybe he wouldn't, but we were already here and I wanted him out of my car.

"Alright, here's five dollars and my number," I said, handing him the money and a scrap of paper with my number.

"Thank you." he said, opening the door.

I nodded and he shut the door and walked away from the apartment complex. I knew I had just been taken for a fool. He saw me as an easy target, and spun some story that I could relate to. I was a bright-faced kid with a flashy car and an inability to say no-a big target. I did learn, though. I would not be taken advantage of again. Next time, I would say no.

I buzzed back home feeling a bit shaken but more capable, and after dropping off the DXM, jumped in the car and made my way over to Louis's college dorm. A quick and familiar drive across town brought me to his college's aquatics center that I had swum at hundreds of times in high school. I pulled up outside, thumping some rap music and puffing clouds out of my vape. He emerged below the street lamp surrounded by swirling snow, toking his vape with a grin and pink cheeks. He arrived and opened the passenger door.

"Happy birthday man!"

"Thank you, thank you." He hopped into the car and I eased back into the college drive.

"You want to do some DXM tonight?"

"Sure, you got some?"

"Yeah, bro, I just went to CVS."

"Nice, how many bottles?"

"Just two: 600 mg. But I had this homeless dude hit me up for a ride outside."

"Slater's talked about bums over there. What did he do?"

"Told me some story about his wife and kids, so I gave him a ride and cash. I got played."

"He probably saw your car and was like I'm going to try to get some money from this dude."

"Guess I gotta pay a price for the DXM," I joked.

Louis laughed and we proceeded to chug clouds and nicotine with speed and adrenaline all the way home. I was excited to have a drugged-out night with my buddy, paired with some weed and celebration of good times. Once back home, we caught up with my mom for a bit who wished Louis a happy birthday. Then we headed upstairs to chill by my computer and begin the trip. We pondered the dosage for a bit, browsing PsychonautWiki and Erowid, before deciding that I would take 180 mg, 12 pills, and Louis would take a full bottle. It was our first time, and so after a bit more research, we popped them with some water. I took a time stamp to keep track of the effects, and then began the wait.

I rolled up a couple joints and took some rips off a bong with Louis while surfing for music and fun visuals. The come up was slow and not entirely noticeable with the weed high until about an hour in. Then, time seemed to slow down, gravity was amplified and the lucid cannabis creativity faded into a disassociated head space. Paired with nicotine, the body high was very pronounced while my mind worked slowly and preferred to be blank. The feeling was excellent, and I was perfectly content chilling with Louis getting baked all night, but then a text from Slater hit Louis's phone. He wanted to celebrate with Louis, and though I was not particularly keen on going all the way across town this late, I owed it to my friend on his birthday.

So, we lined up a ride and after a bit of difficulty navigating down the staircase, sauntered to the living room and plopped down on the couch. After just a minute, our Uber driver pulled up in a grey Dodge Charger. I could not seem to remember the walk from the house to the back seat, but then we were cruising down the road, past the shadows cast by the streetlights on the tall sycamores.

Our driver was a young Black man, maybe in his mid twenties, and I was quite curious about what model Charger this was. I asked if it was the V6 or V8 model, and he seemed very confused. I wondered if the drugs were making me sound crazy, so I looked to Louis for affirmation. He asked the driver the same question in a different way which prompted more uncomfortable silence, and then it became apparent that there was an obvious language barrier. No matter; Ubering was a great job choice for someone new to the country.

The drive was relatively stress-free until we made it into downtown, where the driver took a bunch of wrong turns and got lost. Louis ended up having to get out his phone and guide us to Slater's house while I uncomfortably watched the problems caused by the language barrier amplify. Not only were we lost, but also paying for this mistake by the mile. Finally, Louis managed to give directions well enough that we made it to Slater's. Despite the poor job, we thanked our chauffeur and got out of the car and slinked over to the sidewalk.

The house looked to be built in the early 1900's. The top was painted barn red and covered in oval siding with chipped beige trim around the windows. Out front, there was a covered brick porch with cigarette butts piled in a rusty tin bucket in front of a picture window with the blinds pulled down. Chunks of brick and concrete were missing from the porch that was speckled with flakes of beige yellow paint.

We walked up to the thick brown door and tapped on it a few times before the sound of unlatching bolts was eventually met with the creak of the door opening. There stood Slater in a gray sweatshirt and polo pajama. His complexion was pale and his diamond colored blonde hair unkempt.

"Hey you guys finally made it! Happy birthday, Louis."

"Barely! Our Uber got lost! I had to map us here."

"High ass motherfucker. Come on in, let's get drunk." Slater turned around and walked up a dark wooden staircase leading to the second floor. I followed behind Louis until we made it up to a straight hallway with a tall ceiling. Immediately to our left was a large kitchen colored entirely the same soft yellow beige. The floor, countertops, ceiling, walls, even the fridge had a yellow tinge. Slater went to grab a couple beers and waltzed back over to us.

"I wanna get drunk with you guys tonight."

"You know I don't drink, Slater," I asserted.

"I know. Louis will though," he said, extending a beer to him.

"Nah man, we're tripping on some DXM."

"Oh shit, you guys are robotripping? Hell yeah." Slater popped the beer and took a big swig. "My roommate's buddy has DMT if you want some."

"No way," I said curiously.

"Yeah man, he got it off the dark net. I bet he'll give you guys a hit." I looked at Louis who had an excited expression on his face. A first DMT trip would be quite the birthday present.

"I don't want to tonight," I said, calming my mind.

"I would be down, where is he?" Louis asked.

"I'll be right back." Slater left the room and went into the hallway while Louis and I lingered in the kitchen. What kind of person would want to make breakfast every day in a place like this? There were no pots or pans, boxes of cereal, or snacks, just a greasy smell and shiny surfaces with beer bottles scattered on them. Is this what most people's kitchens look like? My mom's is a third of the size and leagues better. Slater said he has roommates too. A *shared* kitchen. Weird.

Before I got too uncomfortable and ran the risk of encountering the other residents, Slater was back in the room.

"He's got some but they're busy right now. Let's go chill upstairs." I nodded and followed Slater and Louis back out into the hallway which led past another three rooms to a tattered door. Slater opened it to a narrow flight of wooden stairs, no wider than two feet. They creaked loudly as the three of us climbed the steep incline and had to duck to avoid some irregular juts. The staircase opened up into a small room with a vaulted ceiling, no more than seven feet high at its tallest point. Immediately to the left was a bedroll and pillow next to a tiny window, and on the right was a big pile of beer cans and whiskey bottles mixed with packaged foods. Four camp chairs were arranged in a square fashion in the center of the room, tucked under the angled ceiling to conserve as much walking space as possible. Ripped black light posters that appeared as if they had been hastily taped up on the walls stared down at the dingy carpet on the floor, and one big window at the end of the triangle looked out over the street. This was not a room-it was an attic.

I followed them to the camp chairs and rested back, wondering how long it would take to get back out to the street. Sitting reminded me of how high I was, and a mild sensation of falling backwards and physical lethargy set in. This house was unsettling. I did not know how many people were in it, I was far from the exit, and I questioned its structural integrity. Regardless, pleasantly disassociated from my emotions and body, I was happy to shoot the breeze with my two buddies. I noticed a variety of paraphernalia scattered around Slater's chair. A baggie with a dozen Xanax bars, three unmarked e-liquid bottles, a tall vaporizer next to a mason jar of weed, and a small bubbler. I knew he had been heavy into Xans after the high school breakup, but after lots of talk of quitting and changing, I was a bit disappointed.

"How are you guys liking the robo tripping? I've still gotta try that," Slater inquired. I looked at Louis and then back at Slater.

"I'm feeling really good but I only took 180 mg. Louis took a whole bottle."

"A whole bottle? How much is that?" Slater asked.

"Just 20 capsules. We checked online and it's a medium dose," Louis answered.

"What's it like?"

"It's kind of like a mix of alcohol and weed with more spaciness. The psychedelic aspect doesn't really come through until the high doses," Louis explained.

"I want to try it sometime, but I know I can't mix it with bars or alcohol." Slater took a big draw off his vape and exhaled into the stale atmosphere before puffing out: "Let's smoke some weed."

I took out the pop container with nugs and a few joints and began the rotation. Time danced by as we remarked on how good the drugs were and joked about the trivial things that used to go on in high school. The higher I got, the less I sensed the environment, and I became more comfortable by the minute. Certainly, if I lived in this kind of place, I would crave escapism as well, so it seemed the perfect situation for Slater who had been running from reality for the past year.

I mean, the idea was great in theory: a cheap place he could rent out that was steps away from the community college. I do not think that was an illusion either. Slater was genuinely interested in pursuing an education in pharmaceuticals, but his drug habit and dismal apartment seemed to crush that. I probably would have been resentful and loathful too if my mom had kicked me out at 18. Not to mention that Slater's mom had just remarried. Slater lost the relationship with his mom very shortly after that, and then rode the fast train towards ruination. I watched first-hand as my best friend spiraled, unable to help him. The best I could do was be an ally, share in the good times, and give the best advice I knew.

A few grams later, I got a bit antsy and asked Slater if I could get some water and use the restroom. He showed it to me at the bottom of stairs, and then went back up to smoke with Louis. The bathroom was pretty small with a tall ceiling and a window that looked out at another dilapidated house. It was not too uncomfortable, but something about being alone in there felt weird. Sure enough, after I left the bathroom and went into the kitchen, I saw two of Slater's roommates were mingling in the kitchen. One was a guy with long brown hair and a backward hat; the other was a thin girl with bleached-blonde hair. They both looked at me a bit confused until I introduced myself.

"Hi, I'm Christian, Slater's friend. He invited me over."

"Hey I'm Jayce, is he upstairs right now?" the man asked.

"Yeah, I was just coming down for some water."

"Glasses are over in that cabinet."

"I'm Vicky," the girl said. I nodded, and then walked to get a cup. The two of them lingered a minute before heading down the hallway towards Slaters door. I helped myself to some water which tasted odd and I could not decide if it was the glass or the tap. Regardless, being alone felt weird here, and I did not want to bump into any more residents who were wondering why I was in their house. So, I made my way back to the staircase and up into the attic.

At the top of the stairs, I saw that all of the seats were taken, and Slater's roommates were getting acquainted with Louis.

"Hey, Christian, this is Jayce and Vicky," Slater offered. An awkward moment followed by another superficial greeting led to more dialogue between the four of them. I was not in much of a mood to talk so I found a space on the floor and texted my girlfriend, finding comfort in escaping my environment with her. I was not completely stable though. We were still in the early stages of our relationship and she was hours away at college. This was the first few months of a long-distance relationship and my love for her seared in my heart. Any thought of not having her always felt bad, but the drugs deluded me into doubt and worry. Rather than addressing immediate environmental issues, or problems with myself, she became the scapegoat for such things.

A few minutes after I had slumped my motor-inhibited body down next to the beer cans upstairs, a slightly balding stranger popped his head up from the staircase

"Did you guys want some DMT?" he asked, looking at Louis and then me. Louis gave a definitive yes, and the fellow disappeared back downstairs. I looked at Louis who had wide eyes and an eager smile on his face, while Slater appeared completely unchanged.

"Are you going to do some, Slater?" I asked.

"No, man, not tonight. I'm not ready." Of all the people who I thought would take an opportunity to smoke DMT, Slater was one of the first. Though, I did remember his description of an emotional mushroom experience in the forest a few months prior, as well as his grapple with addiction. Far into alcohol and benzos, DMT may have given him a better perspective on the abuse, but I do not think he was ready to handle that trip. He may have known deep down that his habits were causing him strife, and that he needed to change them before taking a ride with the spirit molecule, lest a terrifying experience follow. Perhaps he was more wise than I.

Twenty minutes or so later, the guy with DMT appeared back on the stairs, carrying an oil pipe, a small baggie filled with what appeared to be yellow sand, and a microgram scale. His eyes were very dilated, and I soon learned that he was on a candy flip, mixing LSD with MDMA.

"So it's five dollars a hit, but it's his birthday so it's free. How much for you Christian?" A realization swept over me. I had exactly five dollars in my pocket. About a week beforehand, I had lost my wallet, and earlier I had figured if I was traveling across town, I should have some money. Sure enough, I had the exact right amount.

"I've got enough for one hit." He looked at me and nodded, and then to Louis.

"Are you ready?"

"Let's do it." Louis carried the camp chair over from the triangular corridor of people and plopped it down next to the man with DMT. I was glad he was going first, and I sat back and watched while the pipe was loaded up and he brought it to his lips. The entire room quieted and watched the lighter flicker underneath the glass sphere as it filled with vapor. Then, Louis took a big inhale and his face grew red. Two, three, four hits and the pipe was taken away. His eyes shut and his head cocked back while he muttered what sounded like a Martian language. He laughed and cheered about the golden visuals, reveling in the novelty.

I could not wait to ask Louis what it was like because he appeared to be on another planet. Then the DMT man turned to where I was on the floor, and after repacking the pipe, handed it my direction. I thought it was to be longer before my turn but the time seemed to be now. Louis was still tripping; I had not shared a word with him. My chest began to feel like my legs after a long run, as if a growing pool of lactic acid was surging through it.

"You seem weary," he said, perfectly observing my emotional state. "Do you not want to do it?"

I thought for a second, figuring the nerves were normal, and at that moment I decided I was smoking DMT tonight. When else would I ever get an opportunity? Everything before had just been an idea. This was where the choice was made.

"No, I'm ready." I paused. "When should I take the hit?"

"When you see a little trickle of vapor in the pipe, take it and hold it in." I held the glass tube in my hand and moved it back and forth over the flame he was holding. The room was quiet and I felt people's eyes on me. The feeling in my chest grew exponentially by the second, and my heart pounded. Then the vapor appeared and it was time. I brought my lips to the pipe and took one big inhale. The entire room was still, and I handed him the pipe before lying down on my back and staring up at a sublime blacklight poster.

The intensity of the drug came on immediately. The world around me seemed to vibrate, and the ceiling and poster had pronounced clear edges and visual acuity. The only thing I could compare it to was the come-up stage of an LSD trip. The poster grew more vibrant and colorful while the sublime sun throbbed towards me, and then I noticed some special words on the poster: "Just let the lovin' take hold." I smiled, and it felt like my entire body was on the brink of falling asleep, almost like I was floating. A purple and reddish hue began to develop around my peripherals, and I could not help but drawl out, "I can't believe this is DMT! I can't believe this is DMT! It feels so familiar."

The DMT man expressed gladness in the positivity of my moment, but then a cackling laughter assaulted my ears. It was Louis experiencing some stage of the trip, and I caught a glimpse of him. His face was red and scrunched and his expression was sinister. Frightened, I quickly sat up from the floor and looked at the man who had given me the hit.

"How long does this last?!" I asked frantically.

"Just five minutes man, just five minutes." I looked around the room in a panic until I made eye contact with Jayce who said: "It's alright man, it's okay." Something about his demeanor calmed me and I looked at him for another few seconds unnervingly and said "Yeah?"

"Yeah, just relax man. Just relax." I had only known this guy for a little over an hour, but his vibe was peaceful and reassuring. He reminded me of my long-time friend Dakota, and though I was still a bit anxious, I lay back down to look at the poster. With Louis's disheartening laughter over and a reassurance that the trip would not last long, I let myself slide back in. In an instant, all of the tightness and sensation of lactic acid in my chest disappeared and was replaced by a profound sense of peace. Then, it dawned on me. Love is the key.

I sat up once again and began quickly texting my girlfriend how much I loved her, and how happy I was to be loved. My heart fluttered and my soul rested easy in acceptance of being in love. Finally, the doubt and worry I had carried with me in the past months was extinguished. Love was all that I needed, and I could not help but smile and hold close to my heart this feeling.

Louis had mostly come down and was sharing his experience, while I kept texting my love and swooning to the feeling. Then, Louis and Slater both looked at me and asked how my trip had been. I shared how much love I felt and how absolutely incredible the feeling was. They both smiled and sincerely expressed how happy they were for me, and the entire room seemed to be filled with love. I did want to see what else DMT held, and I looked to the man who had given it to me and asked, "Can we do more?"

"No, you've got a tolerance to it now. You have to wait until another day." My curiosity was there, but I was not disappointed, only happy to share with everyone the great love I felt, and how much truth the saying "Love is all we got" holds.

The small party in the attic began to disperse as people headed back into their rooms, and then as the clock grew close to 3 am, I told Louis I was ready to head home. Slater wanted to come along, though, and continue celebrating, so we called an Uber and waited outside on the crumbling porch. Our ride pulled up in a matter of minutes-a blue PT Cruiser. Slater sat in the front and conversed extensively with the driver who struck me as judgmental, and Louis chimed in. I was happy being quiet, and felt a bit ostracized by my friends, but I knew this uncomfortable moment would be short lived.

We ended up getting to my house around 3:30am, but the party was not over. The three of us went down into the basement and proceeded to consume tons of weed and stare at the tie-dyed mandala tapestry that had been the recording location for all sorts of my trip reports on Youtube. This was truly the golden drug time of the night. Not only did I have an afterglow from DMT, but I was still tripping on DXM, buzzed from the incessant vaping, and many levels deep into the marijuana high. I loved wandering space with my two friends, unconcerned with anything but having an amazing time and savoring every second of our loaded night.

    Six-thirty am came around quickly and I could not go anymore. I told my two friends I had to call it a night, and after they wished me a deep sleep, I went upstairs and immediately passed out in bed. Sleep was sublime but absolutely blank-no memorable dreams or psychedelic visions. When the morning came, my two friends began to pack up, and after some morning coffee and smiles and memories, we loaded up in the car, and I took them back home.

    I did not have a hangover from all the drugs, just a lingering weed high from the night before. The DMT afterglow was simply divine, and everything was a bit brighter because of it. I did not feel anxious or worried having woken up late, but rather a peace and love and joy in the long-lasting memory of the night with my two friends. This experience blessed me with a deeper understanding of love in my relationship, and a realization of the beauty and power of being in the presence of a group of people.

Chapter 12

A Dangerous Endeavor

The time was around 2:30am one Sunday morning, and I had just picked up 36 rolls of toilet paper with Heub and Bo. We were sitting in Heub's black Jeep, trying to figure out who to get. This was the hardest part of the prank: many of our student targets lived unreasonable distances away, and as seniors, we had already tp'ed everyone close to campus. The best tool we had was the school phone book, a compiled list of all of our classmates, address and phone number included. We all knew different people and had different motives, but before committing our arsenal of toilet paper to a house, there had to be universal agreement. It was go hard or go home, regardless of the victim.

Page by page, I flipped through the phone book, holding it out from the back seat for my two friends to see. The propositions had been lackluster thus far and, with the night ticking away, we had to find someone soon.

"We could get that guy by school again," I proposed half-heartedly.

"We've already gotten him three times. It's hardly funny anymore," Heub responded.

"Yeah, we need to get someone we haven't gotten before. Something big." Bo said.

I was on my second flip through the phone book when I spotted a name I had seen the first time through but figured was too risky to share.

"What about my ex?" I offered facetiously.

There was a long moment of silence while the three of us looked at each other, and then Heub said, "That would be legendary."

"Her bitch ass probably lives far out on the rich side of town, though," Bo said.

"If we got her good, it would be absolutely worth the drive," Heub countered.

I continued flipping through the book while the dream of getting that girl danced in my mind. None of the other names read nearly as thrilling as hers, and the thought became real and intimate. There was no way we were actually doing this. Still, my heart raced as I considered the proposition. I knew we were a pretty adept trio of pranksters and had many stories to prove it, but something this big was out of our league.

I tossed out a few more names to no avail before coming upon hers again. This time, it felt real. I paused for a moment and then proposed it once more. Silence and grins followed.

"If we are serious about doing this, we have to plan it," I said.

My two friends nodded, and then we rode a short ways back to my house where I booted up the computer and pulled up an aerial on Google maps. We immediately realized that she lived in a gated community, a known detail I had left out in the initial phase. The gate would definitely be locked, so that meant we would have to walk. Distance meant danger; no one wanted to be far away from the car when pranking. I familiarized myself with the overhead image and some landmarks before noticing a church Heub was already pointing to.

"We're gonna have to park there and walk," he said concisely.

My fingers traced a path from the church to her house, and I pointed to the one I carefully remembered.

"That's hers right there."

Silence followed. I turned to see Heub staring at me with a cold look of doubt.

"That's a long way from the car," Heub said. "If someone calls the cops, we are fucked." I did not let his fear defeat me, and looked to Bo for another opinion.

"It's high stakes, but it would be legendary, Heub. We're doing this," Bo asserted.

"We've never done something this big." I added. "If there's a night to do it, it's this one."

"Let's look back at the phone book and see if anyone's closer." Heub said, reaching for the splayed addresses.

"Let's get your ex, Heub!" Bo said coarsely.

"No way! She would totally know it's us. Plus, we already got her a few months ago. Remember that picture she shared?"

"We barely got her! If only she knew." I joked.

"Let's do Christians ex. Otherwise, we're not gonna do anything tonight," Bo said sternly. He was not wrong. If we were to waste any more time, our mental acuity and motivation would dwindle, and the night would be written off as a loss. We already had the toilet paper, the target, and map. The only thing left was to pull the trigger.

"Alrighty, let's do it then," Heub conceded. A small pit dropped into my stomach as he said this, now, with the possibility of this prank actually happening. I carefully studied the map for a few more minutes with my friends before realizing that it was now or never. We checked for universal understanding, and after shutting the computer off, grabbed some dark clothing from my closet and walked out to the car.

The journey was quiet, 15 minutes of anticipation and digestion of the mission. We had had many big ideas throughout our nights of cruising through school neighborhoods and by classmates' houses, but most were just fantasies. There was a huge difference between talking about doing something and actually going through with it. Even if we had a plan to tp someone, bought the paper, and were sitting just outside their house, sometimes doubt would get the better of us. Many nights ended with Gamecube, cigars, and soda instead of any victims and tales to tell.

Even in these moments, the quest did not feel real. We were just driving down the familiar main street, passing closed smoke shops and neon diners. Not until we had made it to the end did the scenery become unfamiliar. My stomach was the first to identify the presage, followed shortly after by my heart rate. Cold white LED streetlights illuminated a curving road through woodland that opened into asphalt. This road lacked the familiar yellow glow of the one back home, illuminated only by the porch lights of houses set far back from the road. A minute later, the gate to the target's neighborhood appeared. Then, the church.

Heub pulled into the large and completely empty lot, parking far away from the entrance and just beside a grassy mound leading up to the private drive. The engine quieted, lights shut off, and there we sat in complete darkness and silence.

"Are we really doing this?" Heub asked quietly.

"It's already halfway done. We're already here. Now we just need to go finish what we started," I offered.

"Let's do this shit!" Bo shot back.

One more moment of silence followed before Bo opened the door and stepped out into the night, followed by me, and then Heub. The air was brisk, and the sky a clear Prussian blue, dotted with shining silver stars. At this moment, I knew I was not over her. That's why I was here, chasing some kind of a feeling from two years ago. Strange and powerful emotions burned inside me while I embraced where I was and what I was doing. She had wanted absolutely nothing to do with me since the end. We had not even shared a word since that curious seven weeks of togetherness, yet I remained delusional, caught up in the maybe. I prayed she felt the way I did: wildly in love and unable to show it.

I was drowning in years of obsession, stung by the memories attached to the places we had been together. Something made me chase that feeling and long to relive those times. The blaze in my chest as I crossed paths with her in school was unparalleled; she was the reason I pursued righteousness. I did not want any other girl; I did not want the dream to die, so I did everything possible to remain upright. From excellent performance in class, to dedication to sports and health, I would not let myself falter for fear that my hope be crushed.

I hid my deep emotions from my comrades, careful to show only the facade of foolish teenage sport and revenge. Perhaps it was not all a bluff though. She had done me wrong and this was a satisfying form of retribution. Still, I knew they could see through some of me, but there was no time to focus on my feelings. Any energy spent figuring out the deep-rooted psychological reasons for being here would distract us and cause problems. The only thing to do was begin the last chapter of our quest: walk the first quarter mile, make history, and get out.

The gate to the community was just over the grassy hill bordering the parking lot, concealed by a row of blue spruces. Young, lollipop-shaped trees dotted the drive up to two cobblestone pillars that supported a thick white gate. I started the trek up the hill, followed by Bo, and then Heub who carried the decorations. Once to the gate, I took one last look back at the car. This was the point of no return. Then, without a doubt in my mind, I began the journey to her house, followed by my allies.

Not a light was on in the neighborhood, but the soft glow of the moon illuminated our path. I wanted to find some kind of cover and drifted between the sides of the road, but we were fully out in the open. Nothing about what we were doing was subtle, particularly in this space. All of the houses were massive and modern with expansive manicured lawns and symmetrical landscaping. No trees or curb along the road either, just fresh asphalt bordered by lush green grass. All it would take for an utter failure was one vigilant neighbor.

Halfway into the neighborhood and fully committed, my nervousness had been replaced with calm. My mind was now fully on my side and it was too late for rethinking. We had to stay safe and aware. There was no way to casually walk through a gated community at 3:30 am with arms full of toilet paper, so we just hurried along, reaching her house rather quickly. I recognized it, too; the memory of a sunny fall day with her standing in the dark driveway paces away from where we were thawed in my mind. This was the right house; even the car was recognizable, so we set up a base camp behind two big trash receptacles on the road and hid the toilet paper from view.

Still seconds passed while the three of us crouched behind the bins, peeking over at the house.

"This is so sketchy, her entire front lawn is open. They could look right out the window and see us," Heub hissed.

"Nobody's awake in there, Heub!" Bo spat. "Give me a roll, I'll do it." Heub tore open the plastic surrounding the toilet paper, handing Bo a big roll.

"Give me one, too," I said, reaching for the bag. I quickly caught up to Bo who was already unraveling a roll around a sculpted shrub on the edge of the lawn. I advanced a few more paces towards the house, wrapping the paper tightly around a young tree atop a mound of mulch. Then I quickly retreated to base camp where Heub was still peering over, followed by Bo asking for another roll.

"Come on, Heub. Let's get that big tree on the edge of the lawn." I said, gesturing with my hand.

"I'm gonna keep watch here in case anybody comes out. Then I can grab the tp."

"Heub, no one in this rich white suburban neighborhood is awake right now. I'll go right up to the tree out front." Bo grabbed two more rolls and swaggered across the lawn towards the front porch. I looked over at Heub who seemed intent on cowering behind the trash bins before grabbing three rolls and sneaking to the eastern side of the lot. There was a tall tree with drooping branches, and by the time I made it there, Bo was already unraveling. I was just about to throw the first roll when I saw Bo spin around and run. I dropped my toilet paper and hauled back across the exposed yard. Heub was already running towards the car and must have put a hundred feet behind him before stopping to let us catch up.

"Bo, what happened?" Heub asked incessantly.

"You see that light in there?" he said, pointing towards the house. I looked closely at the front window and noticed a whitish blue glow; I could not make sense of it. It did not look like a lamp or flashlight, so I told my two friends I would check it out. Keeping my eyes locked on the window for any signs of movement, I carefully led them back towards the bins. I nodded as they hid behind them and then slowly crept up the lawn towards the porch.

The closer I got, the more the familiar smoldering sensation between my ribs grew. What if it was her in there, staring out at me in her yard at 3 am? I savored the immoral sweetness in being just inches away from where my ex lived. Still, the threat of someone standing there and calling the cops loomed; I was entirely vulnerable. I prowled towards the window a low profile, ready to dash on a dime. Everything was clear. My passion and excitement bubbled while stealth and awareness guided me. My vision was sharp, my body fine tuned. Any sound that broke the silence was immediately analyzed, and I was truly in the present moment.

The intensity grew by the second until I was just close enough to see that the light was only a computer monitor. Relieved, but oddly disappointed it was not her standing there, I confidently walked back to my friends.

"It's just a screen saver. We're good to go. Grab some more and let's decorate."

Then we really began to lay it on. Heub started slowly, running circles around the front bush with a big grin until not a fleck of green showed through. Bo worked with me on the big eastern tree, utilizing our trio's perfected method of application: holding the roll with the tail over our knuckles. We would chuck it high up into the tree, and then watch it gracefully bump down through the branches, trailed by pure white ribbons. This technique covered the most amount of surface area and worked best with a high tear off point to prevent the paper from being easily taken down.

Bo and I must have put a dozen rolls into the tree before taking a look at the rest of the lot, realizing there was more to cover. Heub danced about like a fairy, shredding tiny bits of toilet paper all over the lawn like a first snow. The easy parts had been done, so the three of us returned to base camp to take inventory.

"I think we've gotten that tree enough now. We gotta get the one right up against the porch," Bo said impatiently.

"That's so close to the house. You and Christian get that one, I'll do the porch."

I nodded and then grabbed another armful of toilet paper, leading Bo up to the edge of the house along the driveway. Heub scurried along the porch, carefully wrapping the handrail and balusters. I worked on the tree while Bo aspiringly threw rolls on the roof, leaving white lines on the shingling. We filled all the nooks and crannies. Shreds littered the landscape and all the bushes and trees were wrapped.

By the time we were down to our last rolls, there was very little left to tp. Bo ended up throwing one a little too hard and sent it soaring over the roof into the back yard-a treasure for the owners in the morning. Heub had done a superb job of blanketing the porch, leaving a delicate bow between both pillars leading up to the house. This was the cherry on top. She could not even walk out into the yard without first going through the woven toilet paper. A masterpiece.

We made our final return to the trash bins, taking in the precious moment of admiration. Every tree had streaming ribbons of white, blown elegantly by the twilight breeze. The bushes looked like wrapped Christmas presents, and the lawn, a winter wonderland. The morning dew would glue our work in, and with everything done, it was time to go.

I was not quite ready yet; this moment was special. Certainly, the idea of my ex and her family waking up and seeing how much work they had to do, and wondering who did it was one thing, but our play was over. We could not tell anyone in school, or even spread a rumor as it would certainly come back to us. The only thing we could bring along was the memory of what had just been done, so I soaked it in, this unique feeling of being outside my crush's house in the dead of night, a night of infamy with friends. How fortunate I was to have it.

The sterling stars and silhouetted pines stood out against the midnight blue sky, floating above an ocean of forest green. The houses were stark but uninviting, occupied by potential witnesses and people I would never know. The air was like no other night-a soft cold filled with magic dew. All of my feelings for her from the past years seemed to be condensed into this night, and now it was time to leave it in the past. I did not want to do that though, nor did I want the adventure to be over, but we gave a ceremonious goodbye. Bo and I shouted expletives at the top of our lungs as we sprinted away from the house while Heub charged full speed at the front. Our operation had been a total success; there was nothing more to do but get home. The only mystery that remained was whether she would wake up and see the elegant decor that night or in the morning.

I reflected as I sprinted through the winding neighborhood with the image of those bins and her house burned into my mind. I could not understand all that I had felt, nor could I have predicted even a sliver of what the experience would be like. It was already in the past, the feeling fading by the second. How fortunate of an experience, and memory to carry with me.

By the time we had made it back to the car, we were all panting and celebrating excitedly.

"We did it! We fucking did it!" Heub cheered.

"Hell, yes!" Bo celebrated. "She had it coming!"

"That was epic. This night will go down in history," I said specially. "This is our pact. We tell no one."

Not an atom of doubt lay between us. Our story was legendary as ours alone, and it would be relived for years to come. With one final look over the grassy mound, the engine came to life, sending light streaming into the trees. With that, we were off into the night, completing the last leg of our journey home. My endorphins and adrenaline were fried, and the ride seemed to be over much faster than on the way there. Heub parked us out front in the shadow of the large sycamore, hidden from the yellow glow of the streetlight. We got out of the car and walked through the front door into sheer relief. Our mission was over, and we were safe without consequences. We tried to hold a ceremony but did not know how to. The shared experience was enough. Calming sleep ended the night at 4am and I knew that closing the story and saying goodbye was better done abruptly than spending time on ceremony; the end always comes with ache.

My feelings that night compared to nothing I had experienced up until that point, though part of me seemed to release the dream I had been holding on to. I had gotten the absolute best revenge I could, and had ridden the roller coaster of emotion that came along with it. The more I reflected on that night, the more I realized that my feelings were not just because of her. No, what made the night special was the setting. The trees and the sky, the landscape and the air, my two close friends, and a dangerous mission. Who were we getting? Just a girl from school who lived in a rich neighborhood. But we had all made it more than that. Heub's caution and careful planning, Bo's aggression and foolhardiness, and my pursuit and reckless preoccupation. In reality, the girl really had nothing to do with any of it. All of that emotion I felt, the idea of her and the dream, it was fundamentally fictional and rooted in teenage fantasy. What is even really special about cloaking someone's house in toilet paper anyway? The feeling it brings, the people involved, the fear of getting caught, and the full immersion in the present moment. If she had been just any other person from school, the night would not have felt nearly as extraordinary. The fact that she was some kind of enigma in my mind, and brought about such fierce feelings, made every detail of the night distinct and special. Even if absolutely nothing I thought about her was true, still, the feeling was unparalleled, and the night like no other.

Chapter 13

Sleeping Dunes

On April 20, 2016, I began the morning with eight of my high school friends smoking weed in my basement. We passed around bongs, bowls, and a gas mask, burning through nearly three and a half grams of weed before school. The rest of that day was hazy, but I reveled throughout it in the greatness of our brazen dealings. I would trade smirks with the participants when our paths crossed in the halls, sharing in the adventure of our stoned trip through classes that was concealed from the administration and nosy classmates. This was one of the only days I had gone to school high, and there was neither a better day nor group of people to do it with. Never again would we meet under these circumstances and share in the profound feeling of teenage rebelliousness stirred with cannabis euphoria and potent senioritis.

Exactly one year after that day, I longed for a similar experience with my friends. Almost a year had passed since I had graduated from high school and, with no academic obligations, I could fully immerse myself in the ganja realm. I expected today to be even better than last year. I had more time, more weed and ways to smoke it, an empty house with my mom at work, and an insatiable desire for psychotropic experiences. On the biggest stoner holiday of the year, I was surprised to find the only thing I lacked was a friend, the most necessary part.

The day was empty and my feelings were not the same. Weed had lost a part of its mystery and had become a condition for time spent with friends rather than a novelty. High school nostalgia had an overwhelming presence that was distorted with drugs, which made the past an enigma. Weed was a piece of it, though, and something about a distorted memory of highschool was even better than actually remembering it. So, chasing the feeling, I smoked habitually, clinging to every emotion I could, burned by pieces of the past. Now, here I was alone on the holiday that was meant for getting high with friends. My love was busy with college, and even my mom had better things to do.

Loneliness came more as a result of my internal dialogue than actual external happenings, as most forms of mental anguish do. I did not want to say I needed a friend, or that I needed help. No, I wanted to be needed. I wanted to be an essential part of someone's day, but my friends seemed to be getting along just fine without me. I told myself I was forgotten and uncared for, and could not see the truth. Instead of wallowing in my feelings, I got in my red Charger and drove off. I had brought along just a few things: a thin cloth sweatshirt and jeans, sunflower seeds, and an old kombucha bottle filled with water, plus my laptop. No phone, but my wallet and keys, a general idea of the roads to take, and a strong determination to get where I was going: Sand dunes on the lakeshore I had been to over a decade ago, three and a half hours away.

How difficult could it be? Less than five months ago I had been 4,000 miles away from home, tenting in the

Grand Canyon. A drive up-state would be a piece of cake, and I did not need my phone. I believed that I had the navigational skills to find my way there, but the real reason I left my phone behind was to engage in some kind of emotional warfare. My dearest love had not been in touch much today, and so I would do the same to her. It was not entirely that simple, though; my phone had become too sticky. It was with me everywhere I went, and I wanted to detach from everything. No one would be able to reach me, or find me.

I drove nonstop for two hours to a town at the halfway point, growing wearier by every mile. What had I done? Pursued a reckless journey and told no one of my whereabouts. I had abandoned my love and my home. The guilt of leaving with no explanation weighed on my heart, but at the same time, I hoped that she missed me. I pulled off at a small Italian restaurant, carried my laptop in, and after buying a meatball sub, sat down to pull up the messenger and get in touch with my girlfriend. Sure enough, I had been missed, but instead of fulfilling my desire to be needed, it produced sadness and self loathing. I had selfishly caused the one I loved fear and worry.

It took us time to understand each other through text; I had to explain myself, and she had to tell me how I had hurt her. No longer did I feel unwanted, but rather like a selfish child who stormed off after he did not get his way. Blessed with a girl who was compassionate and loving, I was warmly forgiven. Nevertheless, she asserted the worry

I had caused her. I danced with my emotions and tried to decide if I was allowed to feel better or not. Now, I knew I was wanted, but that feeling came at the expense of my loved ones feelings. I had to bear the full responsibility and guilt for my actions, and affirm to myself that her love would not suddenly change, even in my absence.

We solved the disconnect and I told her my plans for adventure, but now I had a choice to make: Continue on the next half of the journey without any means of communication, or turn around and go home, having figured out the pain that had driven me here in the first place. I wanted to see the dunes and I told her this, so with a great warning of caution, she wished me the best. It did not seem that much further; I was already over halfway there. I mapped the roads to the park on my laptop, sparing myself the trouble of getting a time estimate or route. Why did I need anything more than a map? All I had to do was turn at a few highways, the names of which I had written down.

I packed up and jumped back into the car, taking the first turn towards the lakeshore. The scenery abruptly changed from human development to a winding road through dense young pine forest. I followed this for another half hour before reaching an intersection I had no clue existed. This road was supposed to lead me directly towards the town of Crystal, but the highway signs were not the ones I had written down. I turned around and sped a few miles back the way I had come, trying to see if I had missed a turn. Once I was certain I had not, I headed back to the intersection and decided it was in my best interest to gas up and go inside to ask for directions. Sure enough, this place saw a lot of disoriented travelers-on the cashier counter was a map of the entire area. The clerk seemed a bit concerned when I shared my plans with her, but she offered excellent help with directions. She pointed out a more simple route than I had plotted, and I quickly thanked her and hurried back to my car.

 I was eager to get there with enough time to enjoy the dunes and sunset, but driving was wearing on me. Nicotine would soothe my bones and anxious mind, so I chugged away on my raspberry lemon orange vape. The highway became more remote with every mile, eventually leading me into a thick patch of fog. My solar plexus tightened and I feared missing a critical turn, but adamantly continued the pursuit. The fog was coming in patches and showed brief and shallow pictures of the landscape that quickly returned to haze. I figured I was in farmland, as wooden split rail-fencing planted in lush green grass bordered both sides of the road. Still, I could not see an inch past the fences, and the fog made everything feel small. For all I knew, I was driving through a winding mountain pass.

 I finally came upon what appeared to be a large rectangular sign, and as I got closer, I saw it read "Crystal." I was relieved to see I was going the right way and turned toward the sign before noticing the speed limit slow. Daylight was running short and I knew from the map that I still had a fair distance to go, but the unfamiliar territory and fog kept me at a slow pace. Soon after turning, I found myself driving past dozens of little cottages packed closely together on a lake. I had no clue that this many people lived here, and while some homes looked inviting, others gave me a chilly feeling. I bumped my speed up past them; they aroused some kind of disconcerting memory of a small square room with black light fixtures and grey furniture. Something about the white curtains pulled back to reveal desolate living rooms with chalky walls and soulless furniture gave me the creeps. I had to leave this town of Crystal.

The lake loop had taken at least fifteen minutes before the green park sign finally appeared in the distance. I pushed the pedal down and sped into the very first lot that sat at the bottom of a huge dune. It was oddly familiar, and I thought it may have been the one I climbed over ten years ago as a child for the class trip. The memory of that day was blurry, but the image of the dunes burned in my mind. I grabbed my notebook and hurried out to begin the ascent. My calves tightened at the sudden workload and I regretted wearing skinny jeans, but pushed all the way to the very top.

To my surprise, another, bigger sand dune towered a few hundred feet in front of me on the other side of the valley. I could not see the top of it from the fog hovering in the air, and a little voice in the back of my head said it would be quite easy to get turned around. I knew these dunes were small, though, so I sprinted down into the valley and then up to the top of the next ridge. I expected to see a magnificent view, but the fog obscured everything.

I was disappointed. I had come all this way for scenic beauty but got only sand and fog. At the very least, I hoped to get a nice overlook of Lake Michigan, and maybe even a glimpse of God. That was the real reason I was here. I had not come all this way to look at sand. I wanted a prophetic vision from the Creator. The spirit of a bear, a voice, or whisper that he was there. So, I began searching from peak to peak, trying to find him behind every heap of sand. If one did not reveal him, I knew the next certainly would. I must have scaled five crests before making it to the highest one, when I stopped and felt some calm. Though unsatisfied with the lack of a divine sign, I wrote "Jesus is Lord" in the sand. It felt good and true, but my journey still seemed fruitless. I guessed no sign could be a sign in and of itself.

Nightfall loomed, and I had a long drive ahead of me. It was time to go home. I knew from past travels that adventure rarely went as expected and that the destination is only a fraction of what the journey is about. I took a meditative moment on the dunes and let my breathing slow before enjoying the last view of the landscape. Then, I confidently retraced my way back through dunes where I expected to see my ascent path. To my surprise, none of the dunes looked familiar, but I figured I was coming at them from a different angle. I knew I had not gone very far and decided to head to the top of the nearest hill to get oriented. I knew for sure I had not been on this one, and after peering through the dense fog, I picked out another hill I figured must overlook the road. I trotted over to it and prepared to descend to the parking lot, only to see no car or road, just more sand dunes blanketed in fog.

I did not want to be here any more. It was getting dark, so I ran back to the dune I had climbed to orient myself. I mapped in my head the way I should have taken from that dune, but when I arrived at the peak, nothing was recognizable. My breathing was labored and my heart was thumping from all the climbing, but then I spotted another sand dune I was *sure* was in the right direction. I ran to it through two deep valleys, ignoring the fact that they were completely foreign before climbing all the way to the top of the promising peak. Bizarre dunes disappeared into thick fog in every direction around me and I realized I was completely lost.

My chest tightened and legs burned while my stomach twisted in on itself. I had to get out of here. I immediately sprinted back down the dune into the valley and charged ahead in the most promising direction. I had crossed another two peaks before coming to a sluggish pace as my hope faltered and breath ran out. My ankles ached from pushing sand and fatigue nagged at my muscles. I wandered slowly and desperately, looking for anything familiar before breaking out into brief sprints as my frustration grew. My blood and adrenaline surged while dusk winds whipped across my face and cut through my clothes.

I had not even considered what being lost would be like. What little techniques I knew from watching survivor shows neither captured nor prepared me for the feeling. The focus of those shows is always on food, water and shelter, rather than the emotional damage created by the loss of sense of direction. The world becomes a lot larger when nothing is familiar, and then hysteria sets in. I had come from a place where all my physical needs and safeties were met to the point where I gave them little mind. Now, everything was on the line. I seemed to feel every part of my body. While my chest heaved and my legs worked ardently, my abs burned and my feet endured pressure. I felt exposed like a carnal creature. My primal nature surfaced, and I knew my fate lay only in my hands.

An opening in the fog revealed the first sign of hope: a hill of vegetation. I rushed to the edge of it in anticipation of being able to see the road, only to have my optimism crushed by a lack of human development. There was no parking lot or road, just a hill of trees leading to an expansive dark forest. I had been staving off panic until now, but as nightfall began to blanket the dunes, the graveness of my situation confronted me. I was miles from my car and would surely succumb to exposure if I gave up and tried to spend the night up here. Plus, I had no water or light source.

"Help! Help!" I shouted, but not another soul was wandering these dunes. Fear ate at me; never before had I been lost in the wilderness. The winds seemed to grow with my worry and lightly dissipated the fog, but this only brought more confusion. Now, I could see what looked like a lake that I had not seen before, miles. I did not have any choice now. I would have to descend into the forest to find a road. Wandering through the sand was wearing on my body, and I knew I would just keep going in circles the longer I was up here. In one brief moment, I looked back out over the sand where the fog had cleared, and a mystical image filled my view. The lake was a deep blue, bordered by rich tones of pink and purple that swirled about on the horizon, flecked with fiery wisps of orange. I took it in for so little time, but that one look wrote itself on my mind. Then, I stood at the edge of the vegetated dune and scanned the distance for any signs of civilization. The only thing in the sea of green trees was a big white barn that made my stomach gurgle, and I figured this was what people meant when they say, "listen to your gut."

    I began my descent on a steep and winding sandy path. My visibility was impaired by the trees blocking out what was left of the sun. With no time to waste, I took leaping bounds down the hill, pushing the image of a bear charging through the forest out of my head. Once I was at the bottom, the sandy path led me to a dirt road with a sign that had a map on it. None of the roads or trails on it looked familiar. I was right between two parking lots, two miles in each direction. This was incredibly disconcerting as I had no clue which one I had parked in, and if I went to the wrong one, I would be walking at least six miles into the night. I knew it would be pitch black out here within the next twenty minutes, so I followed the dirt road up to a narrow paved trail winding through a marshy lowland.

The sound of frogs and marsh birds asserted the ominous fact of nightfall as I hurried down the path. Thick walls of plant life bordered my route. I had no sense of direction, so I started running. Fatigue ate at me, but I knew my chances of finding the way back to my car would go down exponentially as the light diminished. The stars grew brighter by the minute, unhindered by the pollution of the city or glow of the moon; tonight would be the kind of dark to extinguish all my bearings. The open main road had to be coming up soon, and with the sounds and lack of visibility tormenting me, I pressed on, running with what was left of the light.

The marsh path wound and finally opened to the 55 mph road I had seen on the map. I spotted the white barn and my heart sank; it was set far back off the road, surrounded entirely by fences and open fields. I would have to blatantly trespass and run the risk of getting shot to get any closer to it. Plus, it looked completely abandoned with no lights on or cars in sight. The barn rescue was a bust, and now I had to decide which way to go. Then, a pair of headlights appeared on the horizon and I beamed with joy.

"Thank God. An Angel."

I stepped out onto the road and saw it was a white Ford Escape, the same car my love had. I waved my arms as the car approached and relief welled up in my bones. The car did not slow down though, and I was not sure the driver saw me, so I stepped out further. The car came closer and closer and I got ready to tell my story as it slowed down. Then, confusion filled me as I watched the car increase its speed and aim to veer around me. I desperately waved my arms and shouted "Please, please, please!" as it sped past. This only made the driver mash the accelerator harder, and then I watched helplessly as the tail lights disappeared into the night.

Woe burdened my soul as I stared off into the growing darkness. I had no idea when the next car would show up, or if it would even stop for me. I knew now was the time to make a decision. Either I would go the direction the car had come from, or the direction it was going. Both ways led into deep forest, but the longer I waited here, the darker it would become. The only frame of reference I had was the memory of the direction of the lake; the picture over the water from the dunes was crystal clear in my mind. I figured people would be close to water, so I went in the direction of the lake and the direction the car had gone.

The asphalt was hard and unforgiving on my feet and the sound of night birds continued to haunt me. I tried to push out thoughts of the eerie reality that I could still be hours out from rescue, and worried about what my mom and love thought had happened to me. The fact that I had almost been hit by a car dawned on me, but I was far less shaken than I ought to be; there were bigger problems to solve. I walked for a few unconfident minutes before making it over a hill in the road and then spotted a gleam of soft white light. I followed the beam to a small cottage decorated with cozy wood and brass light fixtures, like something out of a Middle Age village. There was a car out front and the potential for rescue, so I walked up to the front door and knocked. After just a moment, a kind-faced older gentleman appeared, and I told him my story of being lost in the foggy dunes. I told him I needed help finding my car to which he happily agreed, and my heart soared as I realized I was not lost anymore. His wife helped him get ready before sending him out with his car keys and glasses. I followed him to his car, entirely vulnerable with no means of contacting help. I hopped in the passenger seat, accepting that I was at his mercy before describing where I had parked my car.

He drove in the opposite direction I had been walking, back past the white barn and into a parking lot miles past it. Sure enough, sitting at the very back of the lot, my red car sat dwarfed by the massive sand dune looming over it. The man pulled up next to it and smiled as I thanked him profusely. After he pointed me in the right direction home, I said goodbye to the man who had saved me who I would never see again. I felt blessed by his kindness and hoped I would do the same for one in need.

With a weathered smile, I watched the man's car disappear into the night before reaching for my key. A wave of fear hit me as I furiously searched my pocket before slapping my other thigh and finding it.

"Thank God!" I said in relief. After running all around the sand and being overcome with panic, it was a miracle my key had not dropped out of my pocket. I unlocked the car and looked at my fob for a moment, wondering if I could have heard the horn if I had hit the panic button. How had I overlooked this strategy and not even tried? It did not matter now, and I probably would have been out of range, but what an incredible oversight. I plopped into the cushy seat and shut my eyes for a second. I had finally made it to refuge and wanted so dearly to unwind, but I still had a long drive ahead of me. I pushed the button to start the car, half expecting her to be dead before the sweet sound of the engine caressed my ears. She had not failed me in the middle of the desert, and she would not fail me now. I palmed the vents, letting the hot air warm my fingers before activating the heated seat. She was my home away from home, and would carry me safely.

So I began the journey back, navigating the first hour of unlit country roads winding through dark forests. Alone through unfamiliar territory blanketed with fog, I focused hard on getting back to the highway. Fatigue and pain pulsed through my body, and the once soothing vape flavor of orange lemon was now stale and unsettling. It had been my company on the way up here, but with what had followed, the association was grim. The rain came just as I made it to the highway, so with white knuckles and a determination to live, I endured the drive home. I shuffled through countless radio stations, trying to find sounds and voices that would keep me awake and soothed.

Finally, after three hours of staring at wipers, water, and asphalt, I was home. I gave God thanks just as I parked, bobbing my head down and giving praise. I had been delivered, so I thanked my vehicle as well, kissing the steering wheel, dash, and front end. Then, I got out and kissed the sidewalk over and over before treading gratefully to the front door of my dark house. I let myself in and opened the door to the upstairs, looking at what would be my last exertion before retiring for the night. The stairwell was surrounded by familiar beige walls that met beach-blue paint halfway up. I grabbed the railing and climbed slowly but confidently up to my room before lifting my heavy eyes to the bed, only to find it hidden in fog. I figured I must have left my windows open, and stumbled through the haze towards my bed. I was twenty paces in before I knew I must have gone past my room. How could I have missed it?

 I turned around and found my way back to the stairs to see if I had skipped a turn when I noticed my walk become a trudge. My eyes widened and I slowly looked down to see my feet standing on a mound of sand. I must have tracked it in, so I walked back over to the staircase to pop my tennis shoes off and deal with the mess tomorrow. As I sat down to untie them, my butt sank into what felt like powder, and I turned to see that I was sitting in another pile of sand. How in the hell did I track in so much sand?

 I stood up to brush off my rear and get a broom, only to find the stairs were now a steep sand dune. As I looked up desperately to find my warm room, I was devastated by the picture of sand mountains dissolving into miasma. The creeping feeling of being lost was like a nightmare that kept on playing. I'm home, in my bedroom, looking around at a safe place. The picture remains vivid in my mind, tied to the feeling. Lost in a haze, hundreds of miles from home, sand dunes blanketed in fog in every direction. No one else around. Darkness looming on the horizon, and my walking growing more difficult with each step. No one was responsible for this but me.

Chapter 14

Senior All-Nighter

Graduation rehearsal took place at a big church with Slater and the rest of my class on a sunny May morning. The two of us had taken off early in my deceased grandma's 2001 beige Toyota Corolla. Slater wanted to get home for a smoke session and some vodka before walking across the stage that night and ending high school for good. I mostly just wanted to play some video games and chill, savor this new feeling of liberation. Classes were all done and my grades were in-all that was left was a ceremony and diploma. Slater displayed a facade of happiness; I sensed that a fear of change burned in him just as it did in me. Neither of us understood the full extent of what was happening. Everything was about to change, yet here we were: a couple of high school boys reveling in a day off. It would be our last. Every single day from here on out would not be a day off of school, but simply a day. How tremendous a change whose gravity was still to be seen, like the tip of an iceberg. How sweet the feeling of coming home from school early on a spring day with my friend with nothing to do but enjoy the time and get high. We would never get that exact feeling again; our teen spirit and patterns of high school existence would be forever left in the past. How much we had wished for this day, and talked longingly about what it would be like to never have to come back. Now it was here in full force, and the final sendoff was a senior all-night event after graduation. The last time I would ever see most of the people in my class, the final time to be remembered.

The graduation and the moments immediately proceeding were exactly what these things are like. Caps and gowns, families and friends, salutations and tears. I was primarily relieved in these moments: all the work was done and I found rest in being able to close the book. High school had been toilsome, boring, tedious, and anxiety-inducing. It was a great blessing to no longer fret over grades or getting assignments in on time. No longer would I be tested on an arbitrary scale, or required to regurgitate meaningless information.

High school had been cliquey. Unspoken rules and social customs poisoned the atmosphere to the point where I became entirely apathetic. No longer would I be forced to be in the company of those I had not chosen, nor would I be involuntarily paired with peers or undesirable groups. I was now exempt from judgment within the teenage social environment, able to seek relationships only with those whom I so chose. The faces would soon fade, as would the people I once knew. Certainly, some days could not go quickly enough, while others ended far too soon.

Once the leather-bound diploma hit my hand, cheers and hugs with family and friends signaled the official end. This was it. The constant looming pressure of academic performance, threats from administration on withholding diplomas, daily baths in the pool of adolescent angst, and the mysterious emotion bound to everyday life at school-done. As ceremonious of a goodbye the long-planned night was, I felt little. Whether that was because of my growing cannabis habituation, numbness from the tremendous amount of work it had taken to get here, or great sorrow in not having my grandma able to attend, I was satisfied but lacked fervor.

To add to my unfeeling state, all of the students broke out thick cigars in the parking lot and I joined in. I was a stoner and this was the final time I could show that, so I puffed away, posing for pictures with Hueb, whispering with Bell about our newbie smoking classmates, and sharing final moments with people who had been part of my life almost every day for the past four years. I even found myself taking a picture with Tor who, shortly after, broke out a glass bowl and started burning some blue lotus I had given him. Everyone thought it was weed and wanted a hit; little did they know it was an Egyptian entheogen.

This happened all before the graduates would pack onto a bunch of busses and head to a local college for the senior all-nighter. By this time, I was already a cigar and a half deep with a spinning head and virulent nausea. I looked to ride the bus with one girl in particular but ended up on a bus with familiar stoners and stuck-up kids I had been with all of high school. Even now on the very last night I would ever see these people, they maintained a dismissive attitude toward me. I found great solace in knowing I would never have to share the company of these individuals again, but also a fond appreciation for all those I had befriended.

Once the bus arrived at the college, I was starving and wanted something to curb the nicotine hangover. I had been told there would be a big dinner and dreamed of a salubrious feast, but the only things available were greasy pizza, doughnuts, and soda. None of it looked or sounded good to me, but I had to eat. The sugar did cut my sickness a bit, and then I went about exploring the event. Graduates and parent chaperones were everywhere. There were games, an electric bull, big bubble wands, and all sorts of activities that produced smiles and laughs. My favorite was bubble soccer though-two teams individually packed into big inflatable balloons who charged at each other. Was there a soccer ball? That was not important. The real fun was in sneaking up on kids I had only known in an academic setting and bouncing them across the gymnasium. Getting hit was almost more fun than hitting, though, and perhaps the most entertaining was watching big football players launch tiny girls into orbit. The whole scene was honest fun and an informal goodbye to classmates. I had only ever interacted with in a "proper" manner.

After bubble soccer, I managed to meet up with that girl I wanted to ride the bus with, and we tagged along together for the rest of the night. I knew her well; we were friends throughout most of high school, and though I found her beauty captivating, she had a boyfriend and was strictly off limits on principle. He had decided to skip the party, though, and she was my best friend here. I had many acquaintances and loose friends at this event, but felt more welcomed and valued by her than anyone else. As a matter of fact, I was having a hell of a lot more fun with her than just wandering around and trying to fit in with a group I did not belong to.

    I stayed close to her as the night rolled on and then decided I would watch while she rode the electric bull. Her curly brown hair bobbed as the machine whipped and spun around, but her strong legs remained glued to the saddle. She had a powerful physique with a full bosom below the face of an angel. Her expression was sassy with a sprinkle of curiosity and she most certainly would not tolerate funny business. Her complexion was smooth and naturally tan, placed perfectly next to full pink lips and brown eyes. They were not just brown though; a star of river rock gold expanded out from their centers into a rich hickory, flecked with streaks of honey. She was a gorgeous friend and, despite nothing more than that, a preferred ally.

    The night moved quickly until a magic show put on by the event organizers started in the big gymnasium. The parent chaperones had been told to round up all the graduates and funnel them in for the event, but neither she nor I were particularly interested. Despite incessant prodding and orders from these parents, we stayed put in the lobby and made it clear that our attendance was optional. What could they really even do? We had our diplomas and unless they got the police involved, we were equal in authority.

Even with that, the rule was nobody could leave the event without explicit permission, and so the real job of these chaperones was to guard the doors. That explained why they wanted to get us into the gym; unaccounted for graduates were potential escapees.

We were ready to go, and had been since before the magic show started, but an aggressive male chaperone was unrelenting in his order for us to go to the gym. Thankfully, one of the slender blonde mothers came to our defense, claiming that we were athletes suffering from junk-food sickness. By this time, the majority of people at the event were in the gym, spare a couple of vigilant guards lingering by the door. A few moments of conspiring with my partner preceded a window of opportunity, and so we just went with it.

We casually jogged over to the exit and then I quickly shoved open the door and snuck into the night with the beautiful girl. She lined up an Uber and then we ventured all the way across the dark campus to where our ride was waiting. I half expected the driver to be in cahoots with our school and report us, but this was the real world where the adults were not unified against the students. As a matter of fact, we were the adults, paying some random guy to give us a ride. He did not ask any questions and the only weird thing was the clanking sound of a wrench in the back, something the girl thought was a murder weapon.

We made it back safely to my house, and I was eager to smoke, but I had to share our defiant success. I texted

Dakota and sure enough he was up at 3 am, so I invited him to the party. Not long after we had made it back, he was climbing down the stairs into the basement, ready to share in getting baked.

After a few bong rips of Blue Dream, Dakota and I were having a deep talk at the Amish table while the girl sat on the ground, running her hand across the soft and furry rug. The vibe was certainly odd, but I thoroughly enjoyed the weed and company while riding the high of what we had just done. What a legendary way to go out-total disregard for authority and ditching the lame graduate party to go get stoned with a gorgeous lady and college buddy. I imagined some kind of roll call at the end of the night where an administrator would read off all the names and find our two missing, shocking the whole class. This was entirely fantasy but a fun idea nonetheless, and I loved what we had done.

Dakota seemed to neutralize any awkwardness with honest dialogue, and this special girl remained preoccupied with her overwhelming intoxication and my Maine coon cat, Angel. I felt an underlying need for sleep as the morning grew closer, and by five am, we decided to call it. Dakota buzzed back home in his silver '01' Chevy Cavalier, high as a kite, while I said my final goodbyes to the girl. I could not have picked a better ending for high school, nor a better ally to share it with

•••

That girl was my love, but I did not know it yet. In retrospect, I realized she was one of my best friends. Despite having a broad social circle and using weed as a way to meet new people, very few remained in my life and even fewer would I trust a piece of myself with. Nothing about this night would have been as special or fun had it not been for her. Quite honestly, I think it would have left a sour taste in my mouth had I gone it alone, but with her, high school had a positive ending. Instead of wandering around the night looking for a group to fit into, I got to spend it with the person I fit with best. I did not need romance to feel happy in her company, nor did I need to be accepted by anyone but her. Everybody else on this night was irrelevant; she was who was important. She was who I shared these special moments with to conclude our high school years with a supreme feeling and great story for years to come.

Chapter 15

It's Changed

A heavy morning smoke session with Louis after a night of the same thing primed a day like no other. I had to take him back to the dorms, so we jumped into the red Charger and cruised. The high hit right as I got behind the wheel: euphoric intoxication mixed with a sustained joy in the comradery. He was my good buddy on this shining Sunday morning. The vibes were marvelous and my mind, happily still.

We had just made it to the intersection of Bresson and Bearston when "Immortal" by Yung Lean came on. The light remained red as the echoed plucking intro built to the drop. Then, gas while the otherworldly arcade harmony played with bass that shook the car. Goosebumps covered my skin and I cranked the volume while revving through the intersection. I then looked to Louis who watched me through red eyes of cannabis magic and a soul of joyous clairvoyance.

That moment stuck with me forever. Something about that bass drop, that high, and that morning with Louis-it was precisely what I wanted weed to be. Never again did I have that same feeling, but the song always brings me back.

...

Weed used to be a novel mystery-clouded criminality and missing information. Then it became normalcy battered in supposed cultural enlightenment. Truly, legalization was all that I had hoped for, but when it came, everything about the plant changed. No longer was consumption to be hidden or growing techniques concealed in shadows. No longer did secret internet forums hold the best information; rather, it was in the public eye. Smoking was not nearly as special because it was not nearly as dangerous, and so more people wanted to do it. Perhaps if the cultural aspect had been left out, weed would have retained some level of mystery. Unfortunately, everything about it was tossed out in the open. No longer could there be pioneers, as culture so heavily impacts one's experience with cannabis. The mysteries behind heavily saturated artwork and psychedelic swirls are gone. Now the associations are all explained, the myths debunked, and a bit of the magic, gone.

The raw mind is where psychedelics, weed included, shine; not in the one preconditioned to an experience. Children, being shown the cultural acceptance of weed, will never experience the particular feelings of transgression associated with its use. The way in which culture moves an individual toward a particular perspective imposes major stereotypes and degrades personal subjective meaning. This particular dynamic is prevalent at all levels of society, and evolves with people because humans like explanations, patterns, familiarity, and consistency.

Dissatisfaction with expectations and a desire for novelty inevitably lead people to counter these facts. I was one of them. Though many viewed this plant exclusively through the lens of medicine, or as a recreational drug, I sought its psychedelic properties. I went as deep as I could, exploring the ganja realm and seeking special truth hidden behind heavy doses. I certainly found compelling ideas, though many were the result of hyper thought connectivity and false pattern recognition. This worked great when I joyfully pieced together the oddities of existence, seeing examples of the interconnectedness of everything. I could not have ying without yang though, and so I also found sinister plots, sad endings, and shocking reasons behind circumstances. Getting high, more often than not, made me feel like I was fulfilling a cosmic cliché, or a preconditioned event that was bound to happen because of the interconnected everything.

Oh, how much more the magic has faded now. Weed hardly even holds a place within culture as a psychedelic. Now it is just a medicine, stimulant, creativity booster, social tool, and sleep aid. I grieve the loss of the entheogenic nature of this plant. Modern man uses science to explain psychoactives, rather than looking into the cultures that have used these plants for thousands of years. Even beyond my nostalgic attachment to my early days of weed, I feel that something has been lost. Native Americans shamanic use of cannabis, Mesoamericans' use of peyote and psilocybin, and traditional iboga use in Bwiti culture-all these peoples have great experience and knowledge to share.

Yet instead of building our foundation of understanding on millenia of experience and the cultural evolutions, we look only through the lens of objectivity. The truth of the matter is that every single person handles these substances differently, and these cultures knew this. That is why they developed practices that were universally applicable instead of rigid assertions from a linear school of thought.

•••

Bell had been a chronic cannabis user since our junior year of high school. This permeated our friendship, and resulted in Hueb and me speaking in private about how this changed the dynamic of our time together. Our evenings used to consist of airsoft wars, bouncing on the trampoline, hide and seek outside in the dark, Call of Duty matches, and big bowls of sugary cereal. Now in the first months of my senior year, Bell smoked just about every time before we would get together, and this rubbed me the wrong way. I did not even start smoking marijuana until halfway through my senior year, and was involved exclusively in research and compilation of significant information on psychoactive substance use. The more I learned, the more accepting I became, until that very night with Slater when I smoked for the first time.

Not long after discovering that my mother was a user, I got an invite to Slater's grandparents' house on a Saturday night. They were out of town and Slater was throwing a party; it was going to be he and Sara, Bell,

Hueb, and I. The event was a bit odd with Slater acting gushy towards Sara, and Hueb arriving two hours late as usual, but I found a degree of comradery in Bell. He had driven me here and I figured we could bounce if things started going south. Regardless, he had some Sour Diesel he bought from Kode for the rebellious teenage smoke session. Before we even got a chance to smoke though, Bell dropped a nug and lost it in the carpet so he and Slater incessantly searched until they were sure it was all found. I could only imagine the heat Slater would get if his grandparents came home to a skunky living room and found a chunk of weed lying on the floor.

    Little of the effects of smoking stood out that night; it was the people that made it so peculiar and special. Sara ended up leaving before Hueb even got there, so I was really able to let loose and get stoned with all my buddies. We did not have much weed, yet the night sustained a positive vibe. This was only my third time, so I immersed myself in the novelty but brought very little out of the experience. Perhaps that too is why it was so special; full immersion in the present moment without trying to carry it over to the next day.

    Morning came early and Bell and I were up before Slater or Hueb. I know Bell and I shared the same level of restlessness in this hostile environment, so we were on the road before 9 am. Sure enough, Slater's mom crashed the party not long after, busting him and Hueb. Apparently she walked in right as he was buttoning up his shirt to leave and then they shared a great moment of "Who in the hell are you?" Bell felt like a tremendous friend from that day on, and we shared hundreds more nights smoking together after.

Everything changed though. Bell went to jail for stealing liquor and then moved to Florida, Hueb went off to college and had no time to hang anymore, and Slater could not smoke anymore from paranoia and decided coke and Xanax were a better option. The nights of rolling grape blunts in my basement and passing around bongs for hours were now history. No longer did we get together to smoke as high school friends looking to explore a purple haze. Never again would we sit around that big wooden Amish table and party like there was no tomorrow. Even if we tried to set a date for the squad to get back together and revel, things would never be the same. Experiences and time had changed all of us, and now our minds could not connect with the same blissful frequency of novelty, carelessness, stoned love, and unmistakable fellowship.

For years I chased the feeling, trying to recapture these times by replicating the circumstances. We had always smoked nonstop, and so I made sure to always dose heavy. I tried getting together with the same people, reminiscing on our times together and convincing myself that that feeling was just around the corner. More weed, more talk, familiar items, plots of hooliganism; nothing could bring it back. That unique blend of teenage rebellion, marijuana magic, and the non stop journey together into the hazy cannabis realm-it would never come back the same again.

These moments were destined to be left to the past, a fossilized gem in my memory. Stories are the only way to go back, but nothing will ever capture those feelings again. Truly, I enjoyed unforgettable moments with weed after this. From road trips to the dope capital with Dakota, to heart-wrenching nights of reminiscence, weed has left a powerful imprint on my life. That sensation is not just THC euphoria, though; the people and the minds of infinity brought together to the happening made the time what it is. The odd thing about all of it is that I never knew which time would hold such a mighty presence in my mind. Seemingly trivial or even mundane moments spent with these people turn into robust sentimental pictures of the past that weigh on my soul as times forever gone.

The only lesson I bring from this is the appreciation of and immersion in the present moment. One must savor every second of such moments, for the law of change assuredly impacts all facets of the human experience, and so times fade as quickly as they arise. One whose heart is weighed on by precious moments owes it to themself to chronicle such feelings, lest these things be lost to the past.

Chapter 16

The Lost Bong Under The Sink Survived

The story must have begun sometime during the spring of my senior year, certainly on a weekend night. Slater, Bo, and I were all together down in my basement smoking weed when Slater revealed that he had magic mushrooms. I was entirely inclined to trip through the night, and so was Bo, but Slater refused. He argued that he had work in the morning and was not in the particular mental space to trip, but I knew the real reason: he did not want to trip with Bo. There had been a particular disconnect between them in the past weeks, clouded further by Slater's excessive benzo and alcohol use. I also voiced being uncomfortable with the idea of the three of us staying up all night, so Slater and I reached a consensus with Bo that we were not going to be tripping. Bo had to be sure he would not be left out, and only then could he enjoy the smoke session and calmly end the night. So, after Bo had left, Slater and I conspired and decided to jump in.

"How much should we take?" Slater asked, chasing around some dried caps with his fingers in the jar.

"Let's just start with one. The last two times have been pretty powerful," I suggested cautiously. Slater proceeded to weigh a gram out for each of us before shooting me a high-eyebrowed look. I knew this meant he was ready, and so taking note of the time, 1:30am, I started chewing. I figured I was pretty safe at this dose, and still entirely convinced that cannabis and mushrooms worked well together. We kept ripping the bong, sharing in the curiosity and excitement about what was to come. By 2:15 I was euphoric, relaxed in my solar plexus and ready to go deep, so I asked Slater to weigh me up another gram. I faced no opposition and the atmosphere was warm and enveloping, so I popped the mushrooms and eagerly awaited the effects from a dose I had never been to.

"I've gotta get some more of these shrooms. I'm gonna hit up my dealer a second," Slater announced, pulling out his phone."

"Why not?"

I sat in pleasant silence for a moment while Slater stared down at his screen before I saw him become visibly upset.

"My manager does not know how to take a joke. There's no way I'm paying him back for his jacket. He's the one that cut it in the first place."

"I know, dude, but it was probably a bad idea to wrap up his jacket in the first place."

"He's the dumbass for cutting it open with a knife. Whatever, I'll just take care of it tomorrow."

Slater then turned on some soft music and set his phone on the table. The vibe was still chill and I had a great preoccupation with the effects. A dolphin poster on the other side of the room against a drab yellow brick wall caught my attention. It had been there for a decade, but its presence had seemed entirely unimportant until now. Years had gone by without me taking note of it, but I certainly would have noticed had it been taken down. The poster came from when I went to Florida and got picked out of the crowd by the aquarist. He had me come up on stage in front of a crowd and feed the dolphins, and I remembered seeing my mom and grandma in the audience, smiling and cheering for me. My grandma was gone now, but my positive memories and joyous times weighed against my grief. The poster reminded me of who I was and now I continually referred back to it, determining the level of my high based on how warped it looked.

I felt no negative feelings and while basking in the novelty and euphoria, an augury grew within. I stood up, shut my eyes, and assumed a battle stance. I placed my left foot and hand forward, and then a fuzzy silhouette of a cloaked figure manifested itself. It was a wizard, and I began a scrimmage by throwing a fireball from my left hand and another from my right. I knew it would appear to Slater as if I were throwing an invisible object, but he was one of my favorite people to trip with for this very reason. I felt zero judgment from him, so I threw at least six more fireballs before extending my open palm that sent a bolt of lightning to finish off the sorcerer. I opened my eyes, utterly euphoric and understanding now why these mushrooms were magic. Slater watched me from just a couple feet away, eyes wide and a grin of disbelief.

"I was wondering what you were doing when you stood up. It looked like some magician shit, so I thought, I'm just gonna let this dude do his thing," he said, entirely unfazed.

"Bro, I was in a wizard battle! Throwing fireballs and shooting lightning! This is awesome!" I shut my eyes again, trying to return to the realm of spells, but the feeling had faded. I sat back down and looked up at the ceiling for a moment, before bringing my gaze down to Slater.

"These mushrooms are amazing. Did your dealer hit you back up?"

"I'm trying to see if he can come through, but I'll message him again."

"It's kind of late for that, isn't it?"

"This dude's up all the time. Even if not, he can drop them off in the morning."

I looked around the basement at the metal ductwork running through the ceiling. It was woven through wooden floor supports and would make an odd squealing sound as the heat passed through the pipes. My eyes followed these through the entirety of the room, but then Slater caught my attention by grabbing his phone and shutting off the music.

"My manager is on some bullshit about this jacket. It was just a prank. It's his fault he cut it open."

"I'd be pretty upset if someone saran-wrapped my jacket too, though, but I probably would have unwrapped it, not cut it."

"I know, right? Now he wants me to pay for it. I'm gonna go into work in the morning and figure it out."

I nodded, and after Slater looked at his phone for another minute, he started the music again and I slid back into the pleasantry of the effects. The feeling was excellent but I wanted more, so bashful and hopeful, I asked, "Can I take another gram?"

Slater paused for a minute, and then a great look of why-not swept across his face. He weighed up another gram for me and a half for himself, and we munched them down. The time was 3am, and I had been keeping track of the timestamps and effects on the notes app of my iPod. I made sure to write down the part about the wizard battle and then decided to look across the room at the drab yellow wall with the dolphin poster. The square blocks seemed to bulge outward and the dolphin poster stretched towards me. This classical effect was supremely entertaining, and I knew for sure now that I was in the midst of a potent mushroom trip. I even began to notice circular vortexes around 3:15 and a rainbow hue that bled in through my peripheral vision. These were all of the effects I had been looking for, and I was absolutely entranced by the distortions and potent cognitive euphoria.

My dose was already into the intrepid range, but my timeline was making the come up very gradual. Five grams was the milestone everybody talked about with mushrooms. It was the dose where things became serious, and I wanted to know what came next. Tonight was already a fun trip, but visions of a high-level psychedelic experience played about in my mind. We had the mushrooms, the vibe was supreme, and the sacred effects of psilocybin were shining bright, so I asked if Slater could weigh up another two grams.

"Man, you're going deep. Hell yeah. Go ahead and pop another two, I'm gonna hit up my dealer for some more."

Slater dumped the dried fungi in my hands. I looked carefully at them for a moment. This was it: the next level right before me. I was ready, so I chewed them up and then took down the time on my iPod: 4am.

I swallowed and my eyes grew wide. The place beneath my sternum percolated and I was fully aware that I had committed. This was the night to go deep, and I knew it was only a matter of time before the trip was going to take me.

"My manager is pissing me off with this shit! I'm going to go in there in the morning and tell him I'm not paying for his jacket," Slater spit out, interrupting my dream.

"You're gonna go in there tripping on shrooms?"

"I'll have come down by then. I've already started a bit."

"You took a half just a little while ago. You're gonna

be tripping for another few hours, dude. Just deal with that later," I said, coaxing him back to the psychedelic realm. Slater then plopped his phone on the table and put on some more music, resetting the vibe.

A few minutes had passed before I knew I was on the verge of something big. I was fully immersed in a natural peace of mind and entirely ready to receive what was to come. I felt like I was in an airport waiting for my flight to the cosmic realm to take off. I could not let this feeling be lost to the psychedelic haze, though, so I tapped the keys of my iPod quickly, tracking important details and feelings I hoped to remember. Then I stopped and watched my glowing hands hover in space before another pair appeared. They were holding the top of the iPod, like a mirror image of my own. I stared at the illusion in disbelief, intrigued but joyed at the novelty.

A second later, I shut my eyes and blasted off. The image of a deity with a multi-pointed triangular head appeared in a twinkling zone of deep space. His body was long and thin, covered with a flowing golden robe. I tried to speak to him but my voice sounded like helium and then my ears were overwhelmed by a robotic "zErAOwUW wUahnyao" noise that I was sure was some kind of interdimensional electronic device. I had never heard anything like it before, and I seemed to float in that space for a very short time before opening my eyes to see Slater staring down at his phone.

"How long was I gone?" I asked quickly. He looked at me with a mildly surprised expression and said, "You were sitting there for like five minutes."

"Weird. It felt like I was in another world."

"Yeah, dude, you're tripping out. I'm trying to hit up my dealer for some more of these shrooms. They are bomb," he stated.

That came as no surprise to me. I swear Slater has been on the same thing for the past two hours. Maybe I'm just tripping, though I guess both of us are tripping. I wonder if he's caught up in some kind of thought loop with his dealer.

"Did he text you back?"

"Yeah, he's going to come through later in the morning. I'm trying to see when, though, so I can go into work and figure out this thing with my manager."

There it is again! He's on that same idea of going into work to figure out that thing with his manager's coat. I don't really have the mind to tell him he's in some kind of recursive thought stream right now, though; these effects are tremendous.

I looked over at the wall with the dolphin poster which was now pushed out yards over the basement floor. The grey, wet skin of the dolphins pulsed like a firm goo and their mouths and eyes flooded my soul. The trip was coming on hard, and I knew now was the time to go lie down and ride the bus into the kaleidoscopic expanse. I had the perfect place: a queen mattress on the floor under the stairs with a sheet with bright orange, blue, white, and yellow stripes. The bed pointed directly at a big mandala tapestry, and I had my headphones ready with some Shpongle to bring me into the next dimension.

"I'm gonna go lie down and trip out to some music, dude." Slater looked up from his phone and said, "right on, man," with a nod, and then I waltzed over to the mattress. I lay down and noted the grainy sheets with what felt like crumbs of dirt, but then put in my headphones and began the song "Shpongle Falls." I shut my eyes and fell back, letting the echoing instrumentals play with my ears before I heard the droning of a voice. I opened my eyes to see Slater standing there staring at me with a dull but demanding look on his face.

I took out the headphones in a bit of a huff and told him I was trying to trip.

"I know, but I was just hitting up my dealer and I was gonna see if you wanted to buy some."

"I'm good, bro. I'll just buy some off you if I need them."

"Alright, cool." Slater then walked away and I lay down and put my headphones back on before I heard his voice again. I shot back up and turned off the music.

"I've got some bullshit to deal with at work with my manager. I wrapped up his coat and he ripped it trying to get it open. Could your mom give me a ride down there?"

"It's like 5 am, dude. She's sleeping and your work isn't even open. Plus it's like a quarter mile walk."

"I know, but I'm trying to get down there to meet with him before they open."

"No bro, you're tripping on shrooms. Let's just chill." I got up and guided Slater back over to the table where we sat and listened to music for another few minutes. I was disappointed and a bit annoyed that Slater was not letting me immerse myself in the high-dose experience, but he was my trip partner and I had to keep him from doing anything stupid. Plus, I knew he was stuck in an unpleasant loop and I was sick of having to hear about it.

Slater picked up his phone from the table again and shut off the music before stating: "I'm trying to see when my dealer is going to come through."

"I know, dude! And you're going to go into work because you pranked your manager."

Slater stared at me with a dim look on his face for a moment and then said, "I told you about that shit didn't I? I thought for sure he would think it's funny. I gotta go in there and figure that out."

I stared back at Slater with a hopeless look and then figured a change of setting might get him out of this thought loop.

"It's getting light out. Wanna hit some coffee?" I asked.

"Upstairs? Yeah, dude. Let's smoke some weed too." I nodded and then climbed up the stairs out of the heavy veil over my consciousness in the basement to the real world of the main floor that felt clear and open. I brewed a fresh pot of coffee and poured two full cups while Slater brought the bong and a jar of weed to the living room.

Upon entering the room, the majesty of the day shone in. Pure rays of light filtered in through the windows onto a beige Oriental area rug detailed with rich royal blue medallions and crimson rectilinear patterns. The richly colored designs seemed to magnify up out of the rug and morph into new patterns. These were some kind of otherworldly, shamanic designs that birthed from the psilocybin experience and held some kind of special meaning.

The silence and my immersion in the rug were then broken by the majesty of a supremely fluffy cat: Angel. She meowed like the cry of a baby and padded into the living.

"Angel." I said with the feeling of honey on my lips, waltzing over to her. She meowed again in approval and I pet her and rubbed my fingers through her majestic coat of clouded gray, muted blues and soft blondes. A silhouette formed around her fur as the light poured through it and I was sure she looked like something out of a Disney movie.

Then the happiest dog in existence entered the room: Roxy. A chocolate brown border collie, her face bright and smiling, she was overjoyed to see me. Her tail wagged and I got down on my knees to embrace her. She licked my face which tickled my soul and invoked joy while I ruffled her silky coat. I hugged her and savored every second of the pure love and smiled widely as the Disney vibes grew by the second. Everything seemed to move gloopy and flopsy and slow like the interlude of music in the movie *The Sword and the Stone* and I experienced pure cartoon bliss.

Slater supported the vibe with love for the animals and world as well, and truly the moment would not have been nearly as special without him. What more should we do as high school boys than get baked on a Saturday morning, tripping on mushrooms and sipping coffee, immersed in some kind of fantastic manifestation of the Disney universe. Then the outside tempted us, so onto the front porch we went, sitting in two steel chairs looking out over our neighborhood. The spring air was fresh and cleansing on my face; the sky hidden by the leaves of massive sycamore trees. These formed into the most amazing pattern I had ever seen in my entire psychedelic exploration. The leaves churned and spun into complex geometric shapes and organic green kaleidoscopic images of pure bliss. At this moment, I was satisfied. This was exactly what I wanted. I wanted intensely spectacular visuals, and what more could be asked for than a tree of unparalleled majesty?

The enchanting morning played on for blissful hours until the time came for us to venture to Slater's place of work. Despite the glorious nature of the day, Slater remained preoccupied with his problem. As Slater, my mother, Roxy and I began the adventure, we passed by multiple houses and serene people enjoying the morning. Not long after reaching the end of the road, we came to a church parking lot and a field of tall brown grasses. On the other side was our destination, so we waded into the sunlit prairie. I basked in the daylight while pushing aside sprigs of wheat, and for a moment I went to the planes of Africa. I was an explorer, a pioneer on a safari on a quest for beauty.

The end of the field came quickly, and then we were crossing a big blacktop. In the distance, I saw the grocery store Slater worked at. Now it was time for Slater to enter and go find the manager he had spoken so furiously about. I let him enter first while my mother stayed outside with the dog. I wanted dearly for her to come in with me, but I entered alone in search of a tasty beverage.

I walked through the automatic double doors, trying to act as human as possible and find a simple product. There was one mistake I could not make, and that was grabbing what I wanted and leaving the store with it; I had to pay for it. I shuddered at the consequences of this mistake, and before I could find what I wanted, I spotted him: Slater's manager. He was wearing a green baseball cap, a plain white t-shirt, and blue jeans. He looked in my direction and fear flooded my being. He had a round gut and just then his entire body morphed into a bowling pin shape; his face stretched across an inflated egg head. I stared at him frozen in disbelief, then turned and ran out of the store. He was a menace, a fearsome being.

I recollected myself with my mother and dog outside, realizing that this hallucination had come from all the negative talk beforehand. Slater joined us shortly after, filled with vitriol. Apparently the interaction with his manager had gone sour, and all the way home, he poisoned our ears with ferocious expletives. Each one stuck like a needle, particularly with my mom present, but the most toxic was that his manager needed to "suck a fat black chode."

Another dose had been on Slater and my mind since the grocery store experience, but Slater was insistent on getting in the car and going to the Arizona desert. I knew for a fact that driving was a horrible idea, but I was still down with wandering around the neighborhood tripping for the day. I had hoped that Slater would solve his work problem so that we could continue our day of intoxication together, but by 9:30, he had to return home. His dealer was a no-show and it was time for the trip to end. I must have been experiencing a combination of a come-down and the absence of my friend at this point, and my feelings deteriorated drastically. I wanted to sleep, but the coffee kept me wired and anxious. I could not do much in this state of mind, much less unpack the source of my anxiety.

I went to lie on the couch to see if I would feel better, but my mind continued the torment. What could I do to make myself feel better if I could not sleep? I could only think of one problem, and that was with my relationship. This was neither my high school obsession, nor my true love who came later. This was a girl who stumbled into my life and then we made it a thing. A host of issues lurked under the surface for both of us, and thus bred great problems with our partnership. She was never fully honest with me, but there was one thing about myself that I knew was a problem, and that was weed.

She did not like weed nor the fact that I smoked it, and I loved her. Therefore, the obvious choice was to eliminate that which was causing the problem. So, I found myself back down in the basement next to a two-foot by four-foot chest filled with all sorts of paraphernalia. Glass pieces, a scale, kratom, a half ounce of blue dream, baggies, blunt and joint wraps, a big glass hookah with some shisha, and even a little weed Hueb had given me money for.

I did not think for long and then picked up the box and loaded it into my mom's car. I nabbed the keys and then drove to our local big-branch store and went inside to search for gas cans. I could not find them. Where in the hell would they be keeping the red jerry cans used to hold gas? I found an employee and asked him "Where are the gas cans?"

He spoke immediately and said, "the gas station…" and I sensed concern and regret in his voice. I nodded and said thank you before booking it out of the store, back to the car and to the gas station. I bought myself a gallon jerry can and filled it up all the way before tossing it in the trunk and getting back on the road. I knew right where I was going: the BMX park, an old abandoned park we would have airsoft wars at that Slater had showed me years ago on a bike trip.

I drove through some ghetto neighborhoods and pulled into the dusty lot next to a dilapidated building covered with graffiti. I opened the rear hatch of the car and dragged the box out onto the ground. Once it was a safe distance away from the car, I doused it in gasoline and threw the rest of the can in the box before throwing a match on it. I looked up into the distance and saw something. I could not tell if it was a mirage or a person, but it looked like some guy riding in a go-cart was heading straight towards me. I sprinted to the car without looking back and then gunned it out of the lot.

The last glimpse I had was a burning black box in the rear view mirror. Was there a person driving towards it in some kind of project car? I suppose I will never know. I returned home without any traffic accidents or criminal charges and went through the rest of the day in a fog. This act did solve that feeling, but after going to bed early, I awoke the next day with a faint memory. Only after some time to question if I had actually done what I remembered could I accept it as reality. Sure enough, the box full of paraphernalia was missing from the basement. It had been neither a hallucination nor a dream, and I even returned to the BMX later to find the burned remains.

    Nothing ever came of it except a story that shocked my high school companions. Most of them had seen the box during our heavy smoke sessions; that was always where the weed came from. Its absence brought many questions, and though at first my ego loved to share this tale, embarrassment and regret came with time. Not to mention the fact that the girl I had done it for was long gone. Perhaps it was not all about her though, weed was becoming a habituation. It had permeated nearly every one of my relationships and was an easy scapegoat for my problems. It had become a part of my personality, and was the only commonality I shared with a large part of my social circle. Quitting smoking would certainly mean the end of some of those relationships, yet my ego wanted to test this. What good were these kinds of friends anyway?

    Destroying the box did not change anything, though. I just bought more weed, more pieces to smoke out of, and more paraphernalia. I smoked for years after this experience, but still wonder if I should have quit back then. I know for a fact that doing so could have saved me from a lot of pain and broken friendships, but at the same time, weed gave me many memorable experiences in the years afterwards. I have no doubt that a lot of them were negative, but I would not give up the moments of magic. Plus, I adamantly believe that my current state of joy is directly a consequence of such experiences of duality, and so forward is the only direction.

Chapter 17

A Really Bad Night

Right around 7 pm on a cloudy Friday night, I was out walking with my stepdad while smoking a pre roll of Tahoe OG. We were at the trough of a hill, passing by a small creek that bent through the grassy corner lot. Two dogs, putting tension on their leashes, pulled us towards green space on the edge of MJ Park. A steep hill of brush dominated the landscape behind houses up to the top of the hill where a cul-de-sac was bordered by a massage parlor and a drab yellow house. This dwelling sat feet from the road, always smelled like weed, had a back yard full of dead grass, concrete, and chain link fencing, and never had the curtains open. Approximately 20 ft of asphalt and sidewalk lay between the end of the cul-de-sac and a path up the vegetated hill and into the park. This was the perfect shortcut to get into the park after hours from my neighborhood, and dodge any nosy police trying to bust us for trespassing.

I followed my stepdad up the hill, avoiding the broken glass, concrete debris, and old chicken bones left along the curb. Moving around a splintery wooden fence, the two of us stepped out onto the parking lot and followed a dirt path along the edge of the house lot onto the narrow sidewalk. A silver SUV hauled by at 50, sending my hair up and the odor of emissions into my nose. I kept up with my stepdad, trying to spend as little time close to the road as possible, before another pair of headlights went soaring by even closer, filling my shirt with air. We had made it past the house, and began our way up the hill of grasses when the sound of a police siren disrupted the droning noise of traffic. The two of us scurried up the hill and blended with the shadows cast by young saplings on the top of the hill.

Wide eyed, I stared as the cruiser got closer and the sound of sirens got louder until it passed the house, flying down the road. Seconds later, the sound of another siren grew louder, and a pair of cruisers rushed past the house and far down the road.

"What do you think is going on?" I asked.

"I don't know."

Two more cop cars blazed past before he said, "Let's go see what's going on."

We shimmied down the hill, and still more sirens blared in the distance. This time, an ambulance went by, headed in the same direction. The two of us and dogs marched down the sidewalk of the busy road, searching the distance to see where the ambulance was going. The sound of the siren cut out, and my stepdad said, "They must be pretty close."

Sure enough, blue and red lights became visible in the distance as we got closer, and my curiosity bubbled. I wanted to see what had happened, and cannabis only made me more interested. The figure of a firetruck was the first to appear, then a white ambulance, and then dark-colored cop cars. I walked briskly towards the scene, leading the way before I noticed something white in the street. I could not make it out, and wondered if someone had been injured in a car crash, and if I was going to see some kind of gruesome injury. As I got closer, I realized there was no blood, severed limbs, or person writhing in agony. Just a thin white sheet pulled over a body, and what I could make out as the impression of a face, leading down to one brown boot poking out of the sheet.

I gawked at the scene, struggling to digest what was happening. Why was I seeing this now, and why was I high for it? I noticed a policeman rolling yellow tape in a perimeter around the scene, connecting it to a wig shop just on the edge of a dark patch of road. No streetlights for at least 100 yards. This person had been hit right on the bridge over the creek where guardrails blocked the road on either side. I had longboarded and walked across that bridge a hundred times; it led off the main road down a paved path into the woods. There was even a yellow sign with graffiti on it painted by Slater.

I stared at the lifeless corpse in the road, without any specific emotion or feeling. The vehicle that had hit him-a silver SUV-had a dent on the left side of the front bumper, but otherwise seemed completely undamaged. The driver must have been unharmed, but I know I would be toiling over what had just happened. A brown object in the road caught my eye, and my stomach churned as I thought it was a severed limb, only to realize it was the missing boot. Suddenly, a feeling of shared humanity swept over me. Something about that boot in the road, sent flying off as this man was killed. I could not quite put my finger on it, but I felt connected to this person. The last boot he would ever wear, left strewn in the street.

Having taken in the scene and satisfied our curiosity, the two of us trekked back down the main road towards home. We shared little to no dialogue, just each other's company that seemed to soothe the stress of what we had just seen. The dogs lightened the mood, joyfully trotting along and sniffing patches of fertilized grass. I was soon distracted by thought connectivity, caused by cannabis. By the time we reached home, the memory of the man in the road was nearly gone, and I was on to the next thing-calling up Heub and Bo to come over and smoke. They were both down, and about a half hour later, at my doorstep. My stepfather had gone home for the night, the dogs were settled in, and my mom was watching TV in her room with a bowl of cereal; it was time to chill.

I chose to kick off the night with half a Northern Lights cannabis edible-a 25 mg chocolate bar to be exact. Bo took a whole one, and Heub was adamant on just smoking, lest the edible live up to its history and cause a foul experience for a novice. I remembered taking a 25 mg gummy just a few hours before, and figured I was at a safe dose and could always take more later. Then, the three of us made our way down into the basement and sat at the large wooden Amish table in the center. The walls were pale yellow painted cinder block, and the floor was gray painted cement. It was one big square with a figure eight in paths that led around the stairwell and furnace, cut in half with stairs to the main floor. It was small, but comfortable. I had spent countless hours down here alone and with friends. From Yu-gi-oh cards to GameCube and Wii, so much of my childhood had been spent down here that every single corner had a story and a memory. From intense games of hide-and-go seek tag that often ended in bloody toes and bruised bones, to adolescent feats of strength in which my Vietnamese neighbor managed to take on two friends and me all at once, nothing was quite like the basement.

Times had sure changed, though. Now I was sitting around a big table with two friends I had known for a decade, packing up a glass bong and stuffing a blunt wrap full of weed. We did not play much tag anymore, or get together for Mario Kart or Super Smash Brothers; it was mostly just about smoking as much as possible and the high that followed. Nevertheless, it was great. I loved times like this with my friends and hazing out the basement and my mind. It was a new feeling, something I had only recently been introduced to. I knew somewhere that these times would not be here for long, so I figured getting stoned with good friends and reminiscing would let us enjoy the carelessness of youth and revel before the inevitable changes came. Admittedly, I did want something more. Weed was certainly novel, but I could only get so high before feeling like I was on the edge of a more mysterious realm that required something different to access it.

Out of the blue, and interrupting the smoke session, I said prophetically, "Let's do some LSD, guys."

Silence. Bo and Heub stared at me with unexcited looks and then Bo said, "I don't really want to tonight."

"Come on. We got nothing going on tomorrow, and I got three tabs!"

"Christian, that stuff is dangerous, bro I'm not trying to be messed up forever," Heub said.

"Dude, no one has ever died from this stuff. The only deaths have been people doing stupid stuff like jumping off a building and trying to fly," I explained.

"I feel like that's some shit someone would do on PCP," Bo cackled, trying to change the subject.

"Seriously, let's do it, guys. It's only one tab, anyway."

"What's it like?" Heub asked. "Do the walls breathe?"

"They like, melt and the colors are really vibrant," Bo said.

"It will be awesome! Here, wanna see it?"

Before letting them answer, I walked over to a large black wooden chest that was filled with weed, glass pieces, kratom, tobacco, a hookah, and a tiny Altoids tin. I grabbed the tin and brought it back to the table.

"Check this out."

I popped open the tin, revealing a small rectangle of folded tinfoil. I unwrapped it and exposed three red tabs with black circles on them.

"That'll make you trip for 12 hours, Heub," Bo said, watching him inspect the drugs.

"That little square, are you serious?" Heub asked as he kept a safe distance away.

"Yes, dude, you just put it on your tongue. We could all do it right now," I said hopefully.

"Naw, man, I'm good for tonight. Bo, are you going to do it?" I pushed the tabs over to Bo, and he looked closely at them.

"You got these from Duke?" he asked. I nodded and then was filled with delight as he said: "Alright, let's do it. Heub, you gotta try it."

I was overjoyed and nervous. Tonight was going to be unique, much more fun than just a regular smoke session. I took a tab out of the tinfoil with tweezers and then set it on Bo's tongue. I did the same for myself, and impatiently waited. I figured I could always take it off if I was to change my mind, unaware that just about all of the drug absorbs when it hits your mouth. After a few minutes of Bo and I peer pressuring Heub, claiming that we were not trying to, and then pressuring more, finally we accepted the fact that tonight's trip was just going to be Bo and me.

I had to tell my love what I was doing tonight, so I texted her and got a fairly concerned response. She questioned the impulsive choice, but spared me a big fuss and wished us all a good trip. With that, I was ready to have some fun. My last acid trip had been so racy, but I blamed it on caffeine. Tonight, I was already mellow from the cannabis, and I figured being in my home with two childhood friends would be an excellent setting. I craved something more powerful-a taste of the divine or a glimpse of the underworld. Whatever it was, tonight was the time for it.

Fifteen minutes after taking the tabs, as we sat in uncomfortable silence around the table, my stomach dropped as I remembered the interaction between weed and acid on a drug combination chart. It was cautioned against and so I quickly let Bo know.

"This is a dangerous combination," I said treacherously.

"What?" Bo asked with wide eyes.

"Weed and LSD; it's considered dangerous on the drug combo chart."

Bo reached into his mouth and took the tab off his tongue. He then looked at it with furrowed eyebrows and said, "It's not dangerous to our health, right? Like we can't overdose on it?"

"No but it could just get really intense with the weed," I clarified, playing with the idea of spitting out the tab. I realized that I had to commit, so I looked back at

Bo and said, "Let's just do it." He put the tab back on his tongue, and with that I decided to throw another half tab on my tongue, squashing out the doubt and committing to a fun night.

Another five minutes passed before I asked, "Does it taste bitter to you?" Bo looked at me again with wide eyes and a frown.

"Not really. Do you think Duke sold you some 25i?" I thought long and hard about what I was tasting in my mouth. There was no strong chemical taste or oddness to it, maybe just a little bit metallic and bitter.

"I don't think he would do that. I bought from him before."

"Maybe not to you, but he was selling it to other people. That's why Kode robbed him," Bo asserted. Heub, having been quiet for most of this time, finally weighed in.

"Kode robbed Duke? There's no way."

"Yes, Heub, he stole a whole sheet of 25i from him at gunpoint." A feeling of panic stirred in me as I digested this claim, but I remained skeptical as Bo was notorious for stirring up drama.

"I mean, I guess that's better than people overdosing on it," I said with disgust.

Twenty more minutes went by before I started coming up, and then Heub suggested going to the local market for some snacks. Everyone was in, so we trotted up the stairs and made our way out to his black Jeep. I sat in the back and was glad that Heub was sober. He could be trusted to drive even though he was a little bit stoned. He had zero experience with psychedelic drugs though, so he had no clue what Bo and I were about to experience or how to support us through it.

A short drive and we were there. I was quickly coming up, feeling the intensity of the drug beginning to set in before the car came to a stop. I watched Bo open the passenger door, but I had something more important on my mind: questions for Heub.

"I need to talk to you, Heub!" I pressed. Bo looked at me a bit confused, but then seemed to remember that I was tripping.

"Well, I'm going in. Do you guys want anything?"

"Grab me a soda, Bo, I'll pay you back," Heub said.

I remained oblivious to Bo, focused intently on Heub from the back seat. Bo shut the door and disappeared into the parking lot while I began grilling Heub. I asked about his family's conservatism, disapproval of drug users, and seemingly rigid schedule. His responses were evasive. He seemed to be killing time until Bo returned to settle the vibe. After a few minutes of unsatisfactory conversation, I saw Bo coming back to the car and I opened the door.

"Christian, what are you doing?" Heub asked me.

"I want to go to the store."

"No, man, stay in the car, you're tripping," Bo asserted.

"No, dude, let's go back in!" I spat, stepping out into the parking lot.

"Stay in the car, bro, stay in the car," Heub pleaded.

I looked longingly towards the entrance to the store, wondering what kind of wacky trip it would hold. I knew I was already starting to lose it a bit, and that my friends really were looking out for me, so I propped myself back into the seat and shut the door.

"What do you guys want to do then?" I asked.

"Let's just get back to the house and play some Super Smash Brothers. Maybe smoke some more weed," Bo suggested.

Images of a fun night in the basement with my friends swirled around in my head and I was excited to see what these video games would be like on acid. I was soon distracted by the motion of the vehicle as we began heading home, and I felt claustrophobic. I tried to roll down my window, but it was locked.

"Unlock the window, Heub! Unlock it, I need to get out!" I said, incessantly jamming the plastic lever.

"Okay, okay, it's unlocked."

I rolled down the window and stuck my head out

into the night air, taking a few deep breaths. As I looked back into the car, I saw Heub adjusting his shoulders to his seat, and began to feel a sinking feeling. Why was he forming himself to this seat? His actions looked robotic, like each time he got into the car he loaded up some kind of program. And if he was a robot, Bo must be too.

Great suspicion bubbled in my mind, and as we came upon a red light, I predicted he would stop, just like a robot. Sure enough, he did, and I knew for sure that these two friends were robots, assigned to keep track of me. I had to tell them that the gig was up, that I knew they were robots, and that it was time to get on whatever the next chapter of this story would be.

"Guys, you're both robots."

They erupted in laughter, remarking about how hard I was tripping. I knew this was exactly what they were programmed to do-delude me into believing that I was just being silly, and to laugh it off to change the subject. Of course, the job of the robots would be to conceal their identities, and this was the most clever way to do it. Especially now that their demeanor had begun to change. The more I asserted they were robots, the less they laughed and the more they acted confused. Of course, what was I talking about? I was being ridiculous. How could I ever suspect these two friends of mine were robots? Doing so would be utterly ridiculous. This was precisely what they wanted me to think.

Heub, still toying with the novelty of his friend losing it, decided to crack a joke. He looked back towards me and said "Yeah, Christian, welcome to the future."

My entire field of vision turned white and then a turquoise matrix simulation of reality appeared before me. My two friends and I were there, dressed in high tech space suits sitting behind a large spaceship control panel. A great feeling that I was an alien who had just taken a rip off a bong and woken up swept over me, and I was now in sober company with two of my celestial friends. My entire life flashed before my eyes: childhood memories, tender moments with my mother, and tragic loss. I could not get over how crazy a trip my life had been. I vividly remembered playing war games with these two friends. It felt like these video games had been an artificial representation of the true reality that I would wake up to after this crazy trip of life was over. I was now awake, and everything made sense.

"Was that entire life a lie?! What is this! How long has my life been that!?" I hopelessly questioned. Then, everything faded back to normal, and I was in the rear of the car, looking at black asphalt and dim street lights with my two friends staring out into the night. I knew for sure that if what I just experienced was not the truth, then robots were the only other feasible explanation.

"Let me out of the car! I need to get home!" I insisted.

"Alright, we're almost home. Then you can get out," Heub assured me. I contemplated opening the door and jumping out onto the road, but I knew that too would just be another path in the system. I knew it would be painful and would cause more robots to appear, so I patiently waited for Heub to turn down my street.

Once we were home, I tore the door open and ran up to the porch. My panic and fear grew. Not only were Bo and Heub robots, but my girlfriend and mother were too. A part of a system meant to keep me blinded from the truth. Every single thing they said was programmed specifically to convince me that they were not robots. Only I was real.

A saving grace could be my girlfriend. She had helped me through rough experiences before and filled my heart with joy and rest. So, I called her and explained the situation. A fierce battle between my looping robot thoughts and her soothing voice of reason and calm filled my brain. She would lull me into peace, only to have my fear and panic take me right back out of it, and affirm that she had to be a robot.

Hours of on and off calls late into the night drained her. She would explain the same things over and over, only for me to sink in and out psychosis, trembling and dreading whatever was next. Eventually, she proposed face timing, and her beauty captivated me and reminded me of the overpowering love I had for her. But, this was fleeting, as the terrible thought-loop of systems and robots saturated my mind. These terrors connected to visual alterations, and I watched as my love grew black horns and gnashing fangs. Her eyes were black, I said nothing-I could not dare tell her what I was seeing. Was she the devil, deluding me, or the one whose love for me would keep her up all through the night?

To my very unfortunate disadvantage, a heavy thunderstorm blew into our area that night. My psychosis grew worse and I sincerely feared I would never be the same. I felt impending catatonia as I anticipated being locked in a psych ward for the rest of my days. Foam bubbled from the corners of my mouth, and thoughts of my impending doom grew with every rumble of thunder. Rain poured down on the house, and I began to realize what was really happening: my time was here. I had figured out the truth, and now the government or whatever power had put me in this system would end me. It would only be a matter of time before floodwaters poured into the basement, helplessly trapping me until I died.

T'was my fate unless I accepted the illusion. The only way I could survive was by forgetting the truth of the world-that it was a system-and just going about living my life like a blind being. I remembered seeing a news story about hundreds of people killed by a hurricane, and I knew for sure that people just like me had figured out the system, and that death had been their reward.

The tightness in my chest persisted for hours, growing worse with every clap of thunder and disturbing realization of the system. Hopeless, I decided to wake up my mom and tell her what was happening. I barged into her room and found her, head buried in the pillows. I told her everything that was happening, my dread and fears of death. Her facial lines were amplified as she listened, and though I felt some sense of safety with her, I also felt shy and afraid.

For a moment, she helped me kick the idea. It was gone and I was free. She explained it all so elegantly. I felt immense relief but still felt uneasy. She suggested I take a bath, so I went into the bathroom and chose to stare at myself in the mirror. I looked crazed. Dried saliva coated the corners of my mouth. My eyes were pitch black with a ring of red around them. My smile drooped. I looked at myself with great horror. How could I have been so foolish to be tricked by my mom into believing in reality when she too was a robot?

I quickly looked away, and fled back into my mother's room. I frantically re-explained the situation, but her solutions no longer brought solace. Each time I would pursue the thoughts of a robot system, death would creep up on me. My mother tried to keep me from this death by convincing me of the system. It was as if reaching full realization of the system brought death, and the ones around me did not want my story to end here. And so they would do everything in their power to convince me that things were real to keep me alive.

For a time, I thought I had died. I lay there with my head on my mom's bed, unresponsive while she shook my shoulder, trying to wake me up. It was here where I sincerely wondered if what I had taken was 25i-NBOMe. This was nothing like my first trip, and with the immense terror, foaming mouth, and seemingly assured death, I figured I could have overdosed. This realization haunted me as I thought about how much my death would hurt my mom. I could only imagine what the pain of losing your only son would feel like.

Approximately nine hours into the trip, my mom ran a bath for me with eucalyptus spearmint soap. She sat with me for a short time, comforting me and helping me through the come-down. The idea of robots continued to jump into my head, like an artillery siege of my mind. When I was finally comfortable being alone, my mom left. My love had gone to sleep per my request, and so I listened to "Somewhere Over the Rainbow" on my phone. I felt like a child who had just witnessed an atrocity. The music made me feel peaceful, as if I were floating with Israel Kamakawiwo'ole through forested mountain peaks and a Hawaiian blue sky.

Morning came like a colorful sky after a storm. I stayed in the bath, clinging to the bit of sanity I still had. My mom came in and told me that my friends were leaving. I wanted to see them but I did not think I was of a sound enough mind to not accuse them again of being robots. So, the choice was made for me, and they were gone without a goodbye. I felt sad about this, not knowing when I would see them again and having lost what could have been a fun night. I did realize that I was almost out of the trip, and that my anxiety was slowly fading, I managed to let my love know that I had partially recovered, and that I was going to bed.

I awoke nearly 12 hours later in my moms bed. It was dark out by now. She fed me, and it felt like the food revived me. Each bite was special, but still I was exhausted. Fearing that consciousness would bring about the same fears as before, I went back to sleep until the next day. This trip had not only taken an immense toll on me, but on my mother and girlfriend as well. I knew my actions had hurt them, but having them to support me in such a difficult time was more of a blessing than I could ever ask for.

The weeks and months following this experience were filled with general paranoia and anxiety. I would frequently be spooked by objects in my peripheral vision, and was overall more skittish. I wanted to figure out why this had happened, so I went through the mental quest of figuring it out.

At first, I thought that my robot conclusion had happened because of my lack of trust for people. I observed traumas in my past such as being abandoned or betrayed by my friends, and I ran through old mental dialogue. I saw the flaws in my thinking, and how they had led me to be a less trusting and paranoid person.

As time passed, I saw this experience as the extreme end result of my thought trains. In entertaining notions of a preprogrammed reality, LSD had brought me to the highest level of such thought. If only those Calvinists subscribing to predestination knew. There is nothing good in following such ideas. No free will means that reality is a system, and of course the logic that follows is how to escape it. As a matter of fact, LSD saved me from years of bathing in this psychotic thought process by condensing it all into one night.

Regardless of any profound philosophical insights, or scars from bathing in the pool of doom, above all, the truth that became clear to me is to be careful with your thoughts. One need not entertain that which is evil, as exploring such branches of infinity changes one's perspective. With perspective change comes eventual action change, and so our thoughts directly affect who we are. Purposeful positivity and a striving for the beauty in the world, despite all of the evil, is nothing short of ideal.

Certainly, I could find evidence to support the theory of robotic controlled systemic reality today. But, because I have been there already, I know that that thought path is treacherous and destroys peace. Moreover, there are many more avenues of thought that can lead to terrible and beautiful places. Foresight can only bring one so far, as many of these ideas can be exhilarating, enticing, mysterious, powerful, and carnally pleasing. Only through wisdom and experience does one develop the meditative ability to not only bring oneself out of these realms, but also to identify origin ideas that should be shunned or followed.

Mistakes are still made though, and with them come figurative "caps" to thought trains. This is why in some circumstances, it can be in an individual's best interest to explore that which is painful, as once they have seen a problem in its entirety, they may develop a conclusion, explanation, and peace.

Chapter 18

Becoming

One thing my psychedelic experiences revealed to me through time was the ineffability of the true nature of reality. Specifically, humans limited perception of reality and the vast quantity of information outside of the immediate five senses. Having experienced many traumatic trips, a major conclusion I drew was that perception was everything. I realized that my experience of life was filtered through the lens of my five senses, and thus I was existing in the midst of a happening without understanding the full story. Another way my psychedelic experiences showed this to me was by presenting a tremendous amount of data that was not specifically relevant to survival.

Essentially, I was falling down a rabbit hole looking for divine meaning, unable to fully perceive that which I was immersed in. I figured this was why the Bible condemned pharmakeia or witchcraft in Galatians-5:19. The experiences presented by certain hallucinogenic substances are transdimensional and hold great potential for misunderstanding. As powerful a tool as they can be for growth and love, so too can they be a vector for evil and hatred. I was far into my journey when I discovered this verse through a community member, but I gave it very little weight. Churchgoers' excessive use of caffeine and Jesus's miracle of changing water into wine both served as ammunition against the claim that psychoactive substance use was sinful. I figured that, as long as one did not harm oneself or others, experimenting with substances was a fun, God-given part of being alive. The problem with this conclusion is the specific effects and diversity of psychoactive substances. Obviously, there is a big difference between an alcoholic and one who enjoys a glass of wine with dinner occasionally. This is true for substances of all types, whether they are used in a recreational or medicinal context. Still, labeling users of a certain substance as criminal while others habitually use a different substance is a disgusting double standard. Preferences and diversity are what make us unique, but rigidity and judgment hold back love and acceptance. Nevertheless, substances can be addictive, physically or mentally harmful, majestic, and absolutely terrifying.

A staggering amount of drugs exist today that were not around during Biblical times, and so drawing any conclusions about what is considered "acceptable" will inevitably contain subjective biases and assumptions. Even using science to identify which substances pose more of a threat than others has shortcomings, so ultimately the truth comes down to intent. One's purpose for using a psychoactive substance is paramount, and I do think this is where introspection can be liberating. An individual views him or herself as helpless to a substance will certainly reflect that, as will one who sees drugs as a fun activity for every now and then.

Whether the purpose is to have fun, numb pain, broaden perspective, or simply inebriate the senses, approach fundamentally changes any drug use. This is true especially for psychedelics. Every facet of the experience depends on mindset, and I knew this going into it. My intent was to find meaning. Instead of focusing on the beautifully raw present moment, I occupied myself with attaining spiritual knowledge or guidance for my life. My trips were not about fun, but rather about what I could get out of them. I was, and remain, a firm believer in entheogens holding great existential value, but seeking such meaning is dangerous. Disturbing patterns and false conclusions are very easy to fall victim to with these substances. Because assertions can be so powerful, these realizations permeate into sober life.

For many, psychedelic use involves walking the fine line between therapeutic and damaging experiences. The goal of therapeutic use is to bring peaceful understanding into one's sober life to improve their quality of existence and alleviate mental torment. Damage on the other hand, results in harmful thought patterns instead. That being said, neither side of the line should be viewed as ultimatums in one's walk with these substances, nor should the conclusions be seen as finalized. The purposeful mind is always working towards greater realization and all forms of experience are tracked on our soul and bring tenacity, wisdom, and understanding.

A major injustice is done to the psychedelic experience if it is viewed exclusively through the lens of its therapeutic and damaging properties, as is solely holding it to the realm of recreational fun. There exists a set of people known as "psychonauts" who seek to explore psychedelics and their own mind for the purpose of spiritual growth and deeper understanding. Of course, unrecognized traumas can surface during any psychedelic journey, but the intent of the user is what makes the difference. Curiosity and a yearning for higher awareness are at the core of these peoples' mission, with goals set for the psychedelic realm. The term "psychonaut" translates literally from ancient Greek to *psychē naútēs* or "sailor of the sou.". That is, they aim to explore higher levels of consciousness, and the reality that exists beyond life.

Magnificence as well as abhorrent realities occur on this earth and in the dimensions beyond it. Extra-human experiences can be reached very quickly by psychedelic use, or slowly overtime through spiritual practices and forms of meditation. Not to be confused with low doses, as the real adventure begins at the next level. This is why the stereotype of psychedelic users being wasteful or lazy with their time is incredibly short sighted, as exploring these realms does not come easily or without consequences. What can be brought back by a pioneer, however, is very valuable and has the potential to cause radical change in the world, be it good or evil.

The weak-minded and ill advised will likely manifest much evil for themselves when experimenting with psychedelics, so exercising the meditative mind is a prerequisite for safety. One should go into the psychedelic experience trusting only their raw meditative mind for guidance. The messages from these realms are for the individual and bring moments of temporary reunification with the infinite spirit. No one owes a claim to another's experience; their meaning, enlightenment and spiritual voyage are all true. No mortal can take what comes from beyond; each unique spirit holds the keys to power. No agency, doctor, government body or critic holds the answers to the hidden secrets of the psychedelic realm. Only the pioneers through individualized experience are capable of channeling such divine incarnation.

•••

Years of retrospection could only reveal so much about the subjectives roots of these experiences. I never did quite figure out why they were so intense, though, as I struggled to find my footing in psychedelics from the beginning. Some could say I was neurotic by default, and the drugs only amplified that neurosis, but by the same token, the argument can be made for the calming effect of these substances. I found many benefits and disadvantages of use, and I ultimately adopted psychoactives as a part of my personality for a time. I figured in order to be a psychonaut, I had to be using an entheogen or a consciousness-altering substance in an entheogenic context, such as weed.

Time and traumatic experiences revealed to me that spending too long in the psychedelic realm can make one miss the beauty that is already here. As tempting and as mystical these places may be, without applying the knowledge, the adventures are soon lost to the past, and as such, treasures left behind. Additionally, entheogens are only one vector of many used for exploring consciousness and otherworldly planes, so limiting one's spiritual journey by exclusively using them is a partiality. That is not to say they do not hold great power and potential for people's lives, but supplemental practice is integral to full realization.

Breaks and time for reflection can be beneficial, but I kept going for about four years. I did not heed the negative signs or patterns, and thus suffered increasingly painful experiences until I had enough and quit. That is when I finally sat down to tell these stories, not only for the sake of entertainment, but also for my own understanding. Sobriety paints a lucid picture of the past and reality, but I cannot deny the subjectivity of such a state and will continue to live in wonder of the feelings I experienced in those times that can only be repeated by experience.

With the beginning over, and an understanding of the early cycles of intensity, now the connection can be drawn to the larger circles that follow. All events are connected in some way or form, and thus the taller peaks and deeper troughs of these loops can be accurately interpreted because of the perspective given by these chapters. The patterns of existence are like looking at a fraction of a hyper dimensional object. There may be conclusions that seem logical with the information given, but with having only a piece of the tesseract, much remains to be realized. The data of these patterns is represented by geometry from higher dimensions that signify the connection between all facets of our reality. Identifying such sequences can shed great light on areas needing attention, and events that were formerly misunderstood.

So here's a piece of my geometry; I'll build more in the next book. Maybe it helped you realize more of yours, or maybe you exist leagues ahead, reading my story like a master watching the disciple learn. Regardless, my story is not over, and so continue the walk with me, for curiosity or expansion.

www.ingramcontent.com/pod-product-compliance
Lightning Source LLC
Chambersburg PA
CBHW030904080526
44589CB00010B/135